P9-DMV-176

The Bruce Lee Library
Volume 5

An Anthology of
Bruce Lee's Correspondence
with Family, Friends, and Fans
1958–1973

Letters of the Dragon

Edited by **John Little**

Charles E. Tuttle Co., Inc.
Boston Rutland, Vermont Tokyo

First published in 1998 by Tuttle Publishing, an imprint of Periplus Editions (HK) Ltd.,
with editorial offices at 153 Milk Street, Boston, Massachusetts 02109.

Copyright © 1998 Linda Lee Cadwell
All photos appearing in this book are courtesy of the archive of Linda Lee Cadwell,
the Estate of Bruce Lee, and Warner Brothers Films.

All rights reserved. No part of this publication may be reproduced or utilized in any form or
by any means, electronic or mechanical, including photocopying, recording, or by any
information storage and retrieval system, without prior written permission from Tuttle
Publishing.

Lee, Bruce, 1940- 1973
    Letters of the dragon : correspondence, 1958-1973 / by Bruce Lee :
edited by John Little.
        p. cm. — (the Bruce Lee library ; v. 5)
    Includes index.
    ISBN 0-8048-3111-4 (pbk.)
        1. Lee, Bruce, 1940-1973—Correspondence. 2. Martial artists—
United States—Correspondence. I. Little, John R., 1960- .
II. Title. III. Series: Lee, Bruce, 1940-1973. Bruce Lee library ;
v. 5.
GV1113.L44L43 1998
791.43'028'092—dc21
[B]   98-37849
                                                                     CIP

Distributed by

USA	Japan	Southeast Asia
Charles E. Tuttle Co., Inc.	Tuttle Shokai Ltd.	Berkeley Books Pte. Ltd.
RR 1 Box 231-5	1-21-13, Seki	5 Little Road #08-01
North Clarendon, VT	Tama-ku, Kawasaki-shi	Singapore 536983
05759	Kanagawa-ken 214, Japan	Tel.: (65) 280-3320
Tel.: (802) 773-8930	Tel.: (044) 833-0225	Fax.: (65) 280-6290
Fax.: (802) 773-6993	Fax.: (044) 822-0413	

First edition
05 04 03 02 01   00 99 98 97   1 3 5 7 9 10 8 6 4 2

Text and cover design—Vernon Press, Inc.

Printed in the United States of America

DEDICATION

To the letter writers

To those among us who understand that, while historians may concentrate on coronations and battles, it is to the letter writers that we must turn when we want to truly understand. Like the journals and private papers of the classic gossips and diarists—Pepys, Boswell, Saint-Simon—the function of letters is "to reveal to us the littleness underlying great events and to remind us that history once was real life." For it is in letters that history and biography meet, to form the most intimate of all forms of literature.

Some have said that the theater is what literature does at night. If so, then letters are what the creators of such literature do and think in the evening of their thoughts. For it is there, in the darkened, innermost recesses of one's mind, well behind the glare of superficiality and trivia, that our passions, desires, and truest selves reside. G. K. Chesterton once described the mailbox as "a sanctuary of human words," adding that "a letter is one of the few things left entirely romantic, for to be entirely romantic, a thing must be irrevocable."

Finally, this book is for the person who understands the true significance of letters; who appreciates the fact that it is upon the page of personal correspondence that the true soul of a human being is revealed and preserved in a fashion that makes them always present, oblivious to the ravages of time. It is here that one finds empathy with what Heloise wrote to her beloved Abelard:

> *What cannot letters inspire? They have souls; they can speak; they have in them all that force which expresses the transports of the heart; they have all the fire of our passions. They can raise them as much as if the person themselves were present. They have the tenderness and the delicacy of speech, and sometimes even a boldness of expression beyond it. Letters were first invented for consoling such solitary wretches as myself! Having lost the substantial pleasures of seeing and possessing you, I shall in some measure compensate this loss by the satisfaction I shall find in your writing. There I shall read your most sacred thoughts.*

— John Little and Linda Lee Cadwell

CONTENTS

ACKNOWLEDGMENTS

Thanks are extended to the following individuals, who gave freely of their time and provided copies of their missives from Bruce Lee for inclusion in this book: Linda Lee Cadwell, Taky Kimura, Jhoon Rhee, Larry Hartsell, Leo Fong, Ed Hart, George Lee, and Adrian Marshall. Thanks are also extended to those who have allowed their letters from Bruce Lee to be published in various magazines and otherwise shared their correspondence with the general public.

PREFACE

PATTERNS

"With every adversity comes a blessing," Bruce writes in a letter to his friend and colleague, Jhoon Rhee. The challenge is to be patient until the blessing manifests itself and then to have the wisdom to recognize that a blessing has been bestowed.

The "adversity" that was a constant companion for most of the fifteen years covered by these letters was simply lack of funds to cover the cost of long-distance phone calls. Up until the last year or so of his life, Bruce was prodded by necessity to communicate his thoughts and emotions in writing—in letters to family, friends, and associates—and what a blessing this has turned out to be! Instead of hazy recollections of conversations, we have a collection of artful writings by a man dedicated to honest self-expression. In his films, the world has seen Bruce Lee express himself through his "martial" art. In this collection, we glimpse the private side of Bruce's eloquence as he bares his soul through the art of letter writing.

I feel most fortunate to have been the recipient of many of Bruce's heartfelt expressions. A wave of nostalgia washes over me as I relive through his letters the small bits of our everyday life together, punctuated by momentous, destiny-changing events. Bruce's letters reflect the course of family life—lots of little business, like who's taking care of the dog, what time does a flight arrive—interspersed with significant drama that shapes direction and growth—the birth of a child, the death of a family member. Not so very different from most people's lives, except for one thing that is evident in these letters—patterns.

Patterns This is the most important thing to look for as you read Bruce's letters. What are the central themes that emerge from Bruce's artful expressions? Can you spot an idea emerging from Bruce's pen like a butterfly escaping a cocoon? Can you watch the idea spread its wings and take flight? Can you observe the idea, perhaps now in a new form, as it comes to rest on a higher rung of the ladder of human maturation? An intelligent plan—implementation—realization. This was Bruce. This is how he made his dreams come true.

In Bruce's own words, here is a sampling of the patterns or central ideas to look for in his letters:

- Gung fu is part of my life—the art influences my formation of character and ideas.
- The goal of my planning and doing is to find the true meaning in life—peace of mind.
- Never waste energy on worries or negative thoughts.
- It is not what happens that is success or failure, but what it does to the heart of man. No man is defeated unless he is discouraged.
- What I honestly value more than anything else is quality: doing one's best in the manner of the responsibility and craftsmanship of a Number One.
- This diligently trained body plus a time-tried realistic faith in knowing that *I can.*
- It is not what happens in our life that is important, it's how we react to what happens.

This last statement has formed a credo in my own life, especially through times of unbearable sadness. Sometimes life is nice, sometimes it is not. But it is the way that we choose to react to the nice and the not-so-nice that ultimately determines our characters.

One's life is mostly a matter of choice, the choices we make in response to what happens to us. Take note of Bruce's choices in his life and the process he employed to make those choices. Keep in mind that these letters represent only a snapshot of the underlying intelligence of the author. In conjunction with the essays, notes, conversations, and interviews contained in other books in the Bruce Lee Library, the total picture of a thiry-two-year-old, highly evolved human being emerges.

"Life, if thou knowest how to use it, is long enough," the Roman philosopher Seneca once wrote. And there is no doubt that Bruce knew how best to use the short life he was granted; whether or not it was long enough is not in our power to determine.

—Linda Lee Cadwell

Postscript

Bruce's native language was Cantonese. He began to study spoken and written English at age twelve. There is a funny story about the first day Bruce attended a school where English was spoken. The students were asked to write their English names. Not understanding the assignment, Bruce looked at his neighbor's paper and wrote that boy's name.

Throughout his life, Bruce thought primarily in Chinese. He even dreamed in Chinese. His grasp of English, however, was excellent. He made a deliberate study of conversational English—an emerging pattern of self-education—and his library includes numerous books on English idioms and expressions. Bruce's ability to write perfect grammatical English was unsurpassed. He once wrote a paper for me in my freshman year of college because I was getting behind in my assignments (a direct result of being distracted by Bruce).

You will not always read perfect grammatical English in his letters because, even though he knew the proper rules better than most native speakers of English, he did not always take the time to construct perfect sentences in casual correspondence. Bruce's thoughts and emotions spilled out onto the paper as, in Chinese, his mind flowed as naturally as the waterfall tumbles over the precipice.

I will give you my heart, please don't give me your head only.

—Bruce Lee

Absorb Bruce's letters through the walls of your heart, not through the mental process of your head.

—Linda Lee Cadwell

Introduction

You are holding in your hands the literary equivalent of Bruce Lee's private photo album. Each and every one of these letters represents a snapshot of events and occurrences that were taking place in his life at the moment he recorded them.

As such, each letter represents a historical milestone in the life of one of the twentieth century's most charismatic and fascinating human beings. This book will allow you to be by Lee's side as he steps onto the boat that will bring him back to America for the first time since he was born there eighteen years earlier. You will learn of his plans, ambitions, and dreams ("practical dreams" as he would call them), which ones he actually willed to completion, and which ones he allowed to pass from existence.

You will be by his side as he begins to introduce to America the then-unknown martial art of gung fu. You will share the deep philosophic wisdom and counseling he offered to gentlemen like Taky Kimura, his most trusted friend and his assistant instructor at his first formal martial art school in Seattle, Washington.

You will witness Lee at his most creative, as he begins to unveil plans to develop his own unique and revolutionary martial art system, sowing the seeds of what would become his martial masterpiece of human freedom and personal expression, jeet kune do.

You will also be by his side as success begins to beckon, when, in the mid-1960s, he is given the role of Kato in the short-lived "Green Hornet" TV series. You will also learn of his dignity and grace under pressure, when this TV series was canceled and Hollywood virtually turned its back on this passionate young man of destiny. You will not see him wallowing in self-pity, but instead keeping busy trying to cheer up his friends, such as tae kwon do master Jhoon Rhee, and students such as Larry Hartsell.

You will also be privy to highly personal correspondence between Bruce and his wife, Linda, throughout the most challenging periods in his life. You will witness the pain of his separation from his family, his love for and soul-deep pride in his children, his delight in finally being able to provide for his family's future, his disillusionment with the "jet set" of the late

1960s, and his feelings, friendships, and experiences with celebrities such as Roman Polanski, James Coburn, and Steve McQueen.

Perhaps above all, you will see firsthand how his dedication to quality and self-improvement resulted in his first appearance in a leading role, instantly establishing him as the most exciting film actor of his era, and how the heads of Western studios, who only months before had condemned him as "unbankable" in North America, were now flying across the Pacific Ocean to persuade him to star in their North American feature films.

You will also experience Bruce Lee in his pensive, quiet, and reflective moments. Writing letters to friends and business associates, he soulfully expresses his wish that humans act humanely, that they be "real," "honest," and "genuine" in their dealings with other human beings.

And, sadly, you will share his last thoughts and hopes, written in what would prove to be his final letter—a letter that is both tragic in its unfulfillment and ironic in its promise—which he wrote to his friend and attorney, Adrian Marshall, only hours before his death.

These are the letters of a great man who accomplished many great things and made a difference in this world. They prove that Bruce Lee made full use of the thirty-two years of life that destiny granted him. They are presented in chronological order in hope that they may both move and enlighten you in a manner befitting the way he moved and enlightened all who were fortunate enough to know him.

These letters reveal that his life epitomized the noble ethos of refusing to accept anything less than his personal best. His life embodied a personal philosophy of daily improvement, of cultivated greatness, of decency, of the recognition of the value of interpersonal relationships, of overcoming adversity, and of the glorious triumph of the human spirit. Finally, Bruce Lee's letters reflect a life dedicated to the ideals of "love, peace, and brotherhood," which—fittingly—happens to be the heartfelt phrase with which he so often concluded his letters.

—John Little

A Chronology of Bruce Lee's Life

November 27, 1940	Bruce "Jun Fan" Lee born in the "hour of the dragon" (between 6:00 AM and 8:00 AM) in the "year of the dragon."
February 1941	Appears in his first film. He is three months old.
1946	In Hong Kong, Bruce Lee begins to film the first of what will total twenty Cantonese-language films before the age of eighteen.
1952	Enters Hong Kong's La Salle College, a Catholic boys' school.
1953	Begins to study gung fu under Yip Man, the venerated grandmaster of the Wing Chun system.
1958	Wins Hong Kong's Crown Colony Cha-Cha Championship.
March 29, 1958	Enters St. Francis Xavier High School.
April 29, 1959	Departs Hong Kong for America.
May 17, 1959	Arrives in San Francisco.
September 3, 1959	Arrives in Seattle, Washington. Enters Edison Technical School, beginning in fall quarter.
December 2, 1960	Graduates from Edison Technical School.
May 27, 1961	Enters the University of Washington, beginning in spring quarter.
March 26, 1963	Returns to Hong Kong to visit his family for the first time in four years.
August 1963	Returns to Seattle. Leaves the University of Washington after spring quarter 1964.
July 19, 1964	Establishes a gung fu institute in Oakland, California.

August 2, 1964	Performs at the International Karate Tournament in Long Beach, California.
August 3, 1964	Begins gung fu instruction in Oakland.
August 17, 1964	Marries Linda Emery in Seattle.
February 1, 1965	Bruce and Linda's son, Brandon Bruce Lee, is born in Oakland on Chinese New Year's Eve, the "year of the dragon."
February 8, 1965	Bruce Lee's father, Lee Hoi Chuen, passes away in Hong Kong.
March 1966	The Lee family moves to Los Angeles, California.
June 6, 1966	Shooting of "The Green Hornet" TV series begins.
February 5, 1967	Officially opens the Los Angeles chapter of the Jun Fan Gung Fu Institute.
May 6, 1967	Performs at National Karate Championships in Washington, D.C.
June 24, 1967	Appears at All-American Open Karate Championship, Madison Square Garden, New York City.
July 1967	Names his way of martial art *jeet kune do*.
July 14, 1967	Hired to appear in episode of "Ironside" TV series, shot in Los Angeles.
July 30, 1967	Performs at the Long Beach International Karate Tournament.
June 23, 1968	Attends National Karate Championships in Washington, D.C.
July 5, 1968	Hired as the technical director for the movie *The Wrecking Crew*.
August 1, 1968	Hired to play a bad guy in MGM movie *Little Sister* (later renamed *Marlowe*).
October 1, 1968	Moves to Bel Air, Los Angeles.
November 12, 1968	Films episode of "Blondie," a Universal TV series.
April 19, 1969	Birth of Bruce and Linda's daughter, Shannon Emery Lee, in Santa Monica, California.
1970	Returns to Hong Kong with Brandon to visit his family.
1970–71	Works with actor James Coburn and screenwriter Stirling Silliphant on screenplay about the philosophy of martial art. Movie is to be entitled *The Silent Flute*.

1971	Begins to collaborate with Warner Brothers on developing TV series, "The Warrior" (later renamed "Kung Fu").
June 27, 1971	Films premiere episode of "Longstreet" TV series for Paramount.
July 1971	Goes to Thailand to film *The Big Boss* (*Fists of Fury* in North America) for Golden Harvest Studios. Movie breaks all previous box office records in Hong Kong.
December 7, 1971	In Hong Kong, receives official word he will not star in "The Warrior"; role has been given to American Caucasian actor David Carradine.
1972	• In Hong Kong, films second film for Golden Harvest, *Fist of Fury* (*The Chinese Connection* in North America), which breaks records set by his previous film, *The Big Boss*. • Forms his own Hong Kong production company, Concord, and makes directorial debut in *The Way of the Dragon* (*Return of the Dragon* in North America); again, shatters all previous Hong Kong box office records.
October–November 1972	In Hong Kong, begins preliminary filming of fight sequences for next film, *The Game of Death*.
February 1973	Interrupts filming of *The Game of Death* to make feature film, *Enter the Dragon*, in Hong Kong for Warner Brothers.
July 20, 1973	Bruce Lee passes away in Hong Kong, his death the result of a cerebral edema caused by hypersensitivity to a prescription medication.
July 31, 1973	Bruce Lee is laid to rest in Lakeview Cemetery, Seattle. His pallbearers are friends and students Steve McQueen, James Coburn, Dan Inosanto, Peter Chin, Taky Kimura, and his younger brother, Robert Lee.

Part 1

DISCOVERING AMERICA

(1958–1963)

1958

To an Unknown Advisor[1]*

November 1958

I think it is very rude to write to you [so] abruptly, [particularly] while I am a stranger to you. So, by this letter, I'm obliged to introduce myself to you. To begin with, my name is Lee Shiu Loong (Bruce).[2] My father, Lee Hoi Chuen, is a friend of your father and I am very grateful that your mother advised me to write this letter to you to ask you some advice. Because you are so much experienced

Bruce Lee's registration card from St. Francis Xavier College, in Hong Kong.

in your subject which you are now studying, and I, too, intend to study medicine or pharmacy in the future, I would like very much that you can solve my problems and I hope that you don't find it troublesome. At present, I am a student of S.F.X. (F.4).[3] I planned to come to the States next year and finish High School, I intend to take medicine. As I am ignorant on that subject, can you please explain to me the qualifications of being a doctor or pharmacist step-by-step?

Now I don't even have the slightest idea of that subject. Do you think I can succeed when, at present, I don't know anything about it? Lastly, with all my heart, I do pray you to keep a close intimacy with me, in future.

Thank you very much.

I am truly yours,

Bruce Lee

---

*Notes for Part One begin on page 32.

Letters of the Dragon

1959

A Letter to an Unknown Friend[4]

April 29, 1959

The first friend I met after boarding the ship, turned out to be an Indian person. We had a nice time chatting. He asked me to teach him Cha-cha. After speaking for a while, he bumped into one of his friends, so I ended up alone by myself. So I returned to a room.

Bruce Lee poses for a picture with his father, Lee Hoi Chuen (left), in Hong Kong.

In this room I met with an elderly gentleman, Mr. Lok. Mr. Lok is a frequent traveler on these boats and he offered some pointers which I appreciated. I also met my school friend's older brother, Mr. Chang. We basically did everything together (we went in and out, activities, and so on, together). This person studies choy lay fut boxing[5] and has a definite interest and admiration for Wing Chun.[6] We even came to agree to sight-see together in Japan.

When you go to the bar for drinks, even Coca-Cola costs money. To me, I'd rather drink faucet water. The funniest of all, is when I went to shower; I didn't know that I could adjust the cold and hot water, so I only turned on the hot and it got hotter and hotter as I was showering until I couldn't take it any more. Then I turned it all the way to the cold water until I got frozen. Later on, when I went to the room, someone instructed me—then I understood that there was a "middle" setting! After I got in bed, I felt my whole bed swaying— very uncomfortable. I hope it won't make me sea-sick.

Right now it is 11:30 PM. I think I'd better sleep early, because tomorrow's breakfast is at 8:30 AM.

Monday, May 4, 1959

"Open the door and you see the mountain"[7]
The problem with the above statement is that if you try to be too direct, things don't turn out properly and it always backfires. The mouth says "yes," but the heart says "no."

Today is Monday the 4th. As the boat arrived to the shore, Peter [8] came to receive me. Thanks to him, he took me on the train from Osaka directly to Tokyo for sightseeing.

Tokyo is really an extremely beautiful city. It's as pretty as any Western country. I've never seen so much automobile traffic, it's non-stop, pedestrians pushing and shoving, and the city is full of excitement.

The very colorful neon lights are constantly flickering and changing, showing plenty of images. Compared to Hong Kong, Hong Kong falls way behind!

After meeting with Peter's friends, they invited me to eat Japanese style chicken and rice—the taste is fabulous. Later on, I exchanged my Hong Kong dollars and bought a pair of shoes (very low price), three thick terry-cloth shirts and some scenic photos. Later on, they took me to listen to a music lounge. After listening to the music, we took the train back to the boat at approximately 10:30 PM.

Today is Tuesday, May 5th. I believe Peter has already gone back to Hong Kong. Now I'm left alone, all by myself with nothing to do. In the afternoon, I will leave the boat with some friends I've met on the boat for a little while to buy some souvenirs. At around 3:00 PM, we went ashore. There were two Americans who live in our cabin room; one is around 30 years old, the other around 25. Both are studying law. We chit-chatted a little while and then I decided to pen you this letter.

Now the boat has pulled out, so I will put away my pen. The reason is because when the boat is sailing, the ocean has become rough with big waves and the ship is very rocky—to the point in the evening there was a dance, but nobody could dance as liquor bottles were falling all over the place. I would think that after getting to bed tonight I'll have a hard time getting up tomorrow. Luckily I brought some sea-sickness pills. Tomorrow, on the 6th, I will only feel a little dizziness.

Most of my dining companions couldn't make it up to the upper deck dining area. Today the band on board asked me to teach cha-cha. After I taught for 15 minutes, there came a life saving demonstration. Everybody has to go below on deck and put on their life-jackets. This is very bothersome!

To Melvin Dong

[upon Bruce Lee's arrival in San Francisco][9]

May 17, 1959

Melvin,
The boat arrived in Honolulu. I'm very disappointed to find out that you guys have not dared to write to me.

Later, in the midst of not knowing what to do, suddenly a fellow passenger carrying a picture came looking for me, saying "Someone is waiting for you down below the deck." By the time I got to the gate I noticed a lady and a gentleman waiting for me, one of them was called "Older Sister" and the other was called "Little Older Brother."[10] Both were sent by the Chinese Club troupe to come and meet with me.

They took me around to many places sightseeing, later on we ran into two people, Chang Ki-ming and Chil Lai Cheung. According to the two people, Chil Lai Cheung has a weird temper, but after I met them, he loved talking with me very much. I know nothing about him other than that he told me he has collected thousands upon thousands of L.P. records. I resorted to saying that in Hong Kong, I also listened to a lot of albums. He also complained of his own shortcoming of being hard to get along with, and how his mistress had sold his Shatin[11] vacation house, etc. Then he proceeded to ask about the well being of Papa. He said that in the future he would return to Hong Kong, given the opportunity. But this individual does not trust anybody at all. He handles all his business personally. Why would he ever leave the whole business behind for someone else to manage?

That evening, they also introduced me to a Mr. Tang. This Mr. Tang person is very wealthy. He and I hit it off right away, like we'd known each other forever. He studies Hung style boxing and loves the National Art.[12] He envies my skill and knowledge of Wing Chun and hopes that I can stay longer in Hawaii to teach him boxing, and to find a school for me to teach at.

Later on he invited me to the World's largest Chinese restaurant and nightclub for dinner. One bowl of shark fin soup is already US $25! I think after eating it this time I, myself, will never have an opportunity to eat another US $25 gourmet dish again.

Tell "Pretty Boy Dog" that I bought two tricks for him. I'll wait until I arrive in San Francisco to mail them to him! But in the meantime, it is alright for you to tell him.

This letter was written and mailed immediately after the boat arrived in San Francisco. I really wish that all of you would write many letters to me so I won't have to keep wondering about you guys.

1960

To Hawkins Cheung[13] in Kowloon, Hong Kong

Posted from Seattle, Washington

May 16, 1960

Dear Hawkins,

I see that I am in your bad books through negligence in writing to you and do not know how to apologize sufficiently for the neglect. First of all, Hawkins, I must thank you for your welcome letter.

Hawkins, I am really truly sorry about your sickness, but, please do listen to me, it's no use to become nervous and fidgety; remember that it won't help but just de-improve the illness. Hawkins, I hope you will be better soon. Meanwhile, take it easy.

I admit that it's good to practice Wing Chun. To be perfectly frank, I practice quite a lot on it nowadays (the wooden dummy has been shipped to me from Hong Kong already). But, as for you, I advise you to quit it for the time being and wait till you get better.

At present, I'm still going to the Edison High school, and will be graduated this summer. I plan to go to the University next year, that is, 1961. Well! I still don't know what I'm going to major in, but when I find out I'll write to you again. Now I find out that all those stuffs like Wing Chun, cha-cha are just for killing time and have a little fun out of it, and that study always comes first. Yes, that's right, your own future depends on how well you have studied.

Now I am really on my own. Since the day I stepped into this country, I didn't spend any money from my father. Now I am working as a waiter for a part time job after school. I'm telling you it's tough, boy! I always have a heck of a time!

I didn't do much for my spare time except studying and practicing Wing Chun (for good, of course!). Now and then, a South American would come and teach me some of his terrific fancy steps and have mine in return. His steps are really wonderful and exotic, and how cute it is! I tell you what, Hawkins, when you get well I'll do my best and draw the steps on a piece of paper and teach you. All right?

Say, you still hang around with those guys, if you see Pip, please give her my best regards. In the meantime, please ask Richard to write me and tell him that I have lost his address.

Well, my friend, lots of luck to you and do get well soon.

Your friend,

Bruce

To a "Dear Young Lady"[14]

The mid-Autumn Festival being over. The cycle of the year once again has brought us to the colorful and sentimental days of Fall.

R, how could we let the valuable but short Autumn days slip away without doing them full justice? I often go to the movies these days. I need them for their soothing and inspiring qualities. So, write me a letter [indicating] which one you haven't seen and I'll invite you to see it this Sunday. That will suit you, won't it, my dear young lady?

With my best wishes for all kinds of luck,

I am,

Bruce

To Dianne[15]

Dianne,

To be fond of learning is to be near knowledge. To practice with vigor is to be near to magnanimity. To possess the feeling of shame is to be near energy.

Love,

Bruce

1961

To Ed Hart[16]

March 1961

Dear Ed,

I am sorry that I didn't write till now as I was very busy straightening up my entrance requirements for the University of Washington. Now everything is all right. I am being admitted for the Spring quarter, which will start the 27th of this month.

Ed, we miss you very much here, especially I, for having lost a good writer. But, of course, it's for our friendship that I really miss you most. Ed, do your best and save up some money and come back to us.

We have given quite a number of exhibitions, and I have appeared on TV twice with Fook Young.

We might give an exhibition on April 8th for the Highline High School. Right now, everybody is practicing hard for it. I have ten students so far and the club is taking shape. Maybe [in] two more months, it will be opened to the public.

I am beginning to teach sparring to the students, and am doing my best to train their kicking technique. Jesse[17] is still the outstanding one among the students, though he is not so limber in his legs.

You know something?—It's a surprise!—I am going to take up judo in the University for the physical education requirement. Shuso is teaching there.

Well! Ed, write soon, and I promise I'll write back on time.

Your teacher and friend,

Bruce

To Ed Hart, Brooklyn, New York

Posted from Seattle

May 1961

Dear Ed,

We were talking about you yesterday when I received your letter. Is it true that you are planning to come back?

Jesse is all right and is now living in Chinatown at the Green Hotel. I guess you know that he has been promoted to a black belt. At present he works for Roy Garcia during the weekend. He is going to Edison now.

I don't have the club anymore; in fact, we still owe $80 for it, as everybody is out of a job and couldn't keep it up. Also, I have stopped teaching as I have to have a part time job to tide me over my financial problem.

The fellows are planning to pay me for lessons which might be able to work out as a part-time job for me.

Ed, one thing I want you to know is we all miss you very much and hope that you will join us in the very near future. I don't know how to describe it in words, as my English is not so good, so I only say that I am proud to have a friend like you and I miss you very much, and I hope that you can come back to Seattle.

Your friend always,

Bruce

1962

To Pearl Tso[18]

September 1962

Dear Pearl,

This letter is hard to understand. It contains my dreams and my ways of thinking. As a whole, you can call it my way of life. It will be rather confusing as it is difficult to write down exactly how I feel. Yet I want to write and let you know about it. I'll do my best to write it clearly and I hope that you, too, will keep an open mind in this letter, and don't arrive at any conclusions till you are finished.

There are two ways of making a good living. One is the result of hard working, and the other, the result of the imagination (requires work, too, of course). It is a fact that labor and thrift produce a competence, but fortune, in the sense of wealth, is the reward of the man who can think of something that hasn't been thought of before. In every industry, in every profession, ideas are what America is looking for. Ideas have made America what she is, and one good idea will make a man what he wants to be.

Gung fu is the best of all martial art; yet the Chinese derivatives of judo and karate, which are only basics of gung fu, are flourishing all over the U.S. . . . because no one has heard of this supreme art [and] there are no competent instructors. . . . I believe my long years of practice back up my title to become the first instructor of this movement.

One part of my life is gung fu. This art influences [me] greatly in the formation of my character and ideas. I practice gung fu as a physical culture, a form of mental training, a method of self-defense, and a way of life. Gung fu is the best of all martial art;

yet the Chinese derivatives of judo and karate, which are only basics of gung fu, are flourishing all over the U.S. This so happens because no one has heard of this supreme art; also there are no competent instructors. . . I believe my long years of practice back up my title to become the first instructor of this movement. There are yet long years ahead of me to polish my techniques and character. My aim, therefore, is to establish a first Gung Fu Institute that will later spread out all over the U.S. (I have set a time limit of 10 to 15 years to complete the whole project). My reason in doing this is not the sole objective of making money. The motives are many and among them are: I like to let the world know about the greatness of this Chinese art; I enjoy teaching and helping people; I like to have a well-to-do home for my family; I like to originate something; and the last but yet one of the most important is because gung fu is part of myself.

I know my idea is right, and, therefore, the results would be satisfactory. I don't really worry about the reward, but to set in motion the machinery to achieve it. My contribution will be the measure of my reward and success.

Before he passed away, some asked the late Dr. Charles P. Steinmetz, the electrical genius, in his opinion "What branch of science would make the most progress in the next twenty-five years?" He paused and thought for several minutes then like a flash replied, "spiritual realization." When man comes to a conscious vital realization of those great spiritual forces within himself and begins to use those forces in science, in business, and in life, his progress in the future will be unparalleled.

I feel I have this great creative and spiritual force within me that is greater than faith, greater than ambition, greater than confidence, greater than determination, greater than vision. It is all these combined. My brain becomes magnetized with this dominating force which I hold in my hand.

When you drop a pebble into a pool of water, the pebble starts a series of ripples that expand until they encompass the whole pool. This is exactly what will happen when I give my ideas a definite plan of action. Right now, I can project my thoughts into the future, I can see ahead of me. I dream (remember that practical dreamers never quit). I may now own nothing but a little place down in a basement, but once my imagination has got up a full head of steam, I can see painted on a canvas of my mind a picture of a fine, big five or six story Gung Fu Institute with branches all over the States. I am not easily discouraged, readily visualize myself as overcoming obstacles, winning

Lee seemed always to have a pen in his hand—even during the filming of Enter the Dragon.

out over setbacks, achieving "impossible" objectives.

Whether it is the God-head or not, I feel this great force, this untapped power, this dynamic something within me. This feeling defies description, and [there is] no experience with which this feeling may be compared. It is something like a strong emotion mixed with faith, but a lot stronger.

All in all, the goal of my planning and doing is to find the true meaning in life—peace of mind. I know that the sum of all possessions I mentioned does not necessarily add up to peace of mind; however, it can be if I devote [my energy] to real accomplishment of self rather than neurotic combat. In order to achieve this peace of mind, the teaching of detachment of Taoism and Zen proved to be valuable. . . .

Probably, people will say I'm too conscious of success. Well, I am not. You see, my will to do springs from the knowledge that I CAN DO. I'm only being natural, for there is no fear or doubt inside my mind.

Pearl, success comes to those who become success-conscious. If you don't aim at an object, how the heck on earth do you think you can get it?

Warm regards,

Bruce

1963

To Linda[19]

Oct. 20, 1963

To the sweetest girl, from the man who appreciates her.

Linda,
To live content with small means; to seek elegance rather than luxury, and refinement rather than fashion, to be worthy, not respectable, and wealthy, not rich; to study hard, think quietly, talk gently, act frankly; to bear all cheerfully, do all bravely, await occasions, hurry never.

In other words, to let the spiritual, unbidden and unconscious, grow up through the common.

Bruce

Notes

1. It is uncertain to whom Bruce Lee addressed this letter as all that remains is his first draft. However, given that he was in Saint Francis Xavier High School when it was written, and upon checking his daytime diary for November 30, 1958, we find the following entry—"Now I try to find out my career—whether as a doctor or another? If as a doctor I must study hard"—it is safe to assume that this letter was penned during this period of his life.
2. Lee *Shiu Loong* (or Lee *Shiu Lung*) literally translates as "Lee Little Dragon" (the surname always comes first in Chinese). This was the "stage name" given to Bruce when he first appeared in Hong Kong films. Bruce's birth name was Lee Jun Fan, and in his early school years he was called Lee Yuen Kam. At home with his family, Bruce's nickname was Sai Fon, literally "Little Phoenix." The English name Bruce was given to him by a nurse when he was born, but he did not use this name until after the age of twelve, when he attended a school where English was spoken.
3. Bruce Lee attended Saint Francis Xavier High School in Hong Kong during 1958, one year before he set out on his return to America.
4. Bruce Lee began to write this letter to a friend in Hong Kong to tell him of his experiences on the boat that was taking him to America for the first time since he

was born there on November 27, 1940, some eighteen years earlier. This letter is fascinating in that it serves as a diary of sorts, written on the first day of his voyage, wherein he records his feelings and experiences on what would eventually prove to be a highly significant journey.

5. Choy li fut gung fu is considered one of the most popular gung fu systems in Asia. It is practiced by approximately one-third of the martial artists in Hong Kong and is famous for combining hard and soft techniques, speed, balance, power, and extension. In her book *The Complete Guide to Kung Fu Fighting Styles* (Burbank, Calif.: Unique Publications, 1985), authority Jane Hallander writes, "Not only does the style contain a vast variety of hand and weapons forms, but many of the top full-contact tournament fighters in Southeast Asia are choy-li-fut practitioners, a fact that supports the art's reputation as one of the most powerful kung fu styles in existence."

6. Wing Chun gung fu is considered highly aggressive. It focuses on centerline attacks, wasting no effort and using blocks to redirect the opponent's strikes, so that the Wing Chun practitioner can counterattack with either his blocking hand or the other hand in a very close-in position. Since the shortest distance between two points is a straight line, there are no "curved" movements in the Wing Chun style that was taught to Bruce Lee. Sixty percent of attacking techniques are hand techniques and the other forty percent consists of short low kicks, hand and foot techniques being delivered simultaneously. Wing Chun was the only martial art that Bruce Lee studied formally, which he did under renowned Wing Chun grandmaster Yip Man from 1954 until Bruce departed from Hong Kong on April 29, 1959.

7. A famous Chinese saying denoting a person who gives direct and frank opinions.

8. Bruce's older brother.

9. Melvin Dong was a friend during Bruce Lee's teenage years in Hong Kong.

10. Bruce's parents had contacts among overseas Chinese in the performing arts.

11. Shatin is an area in Hong Kong's New Territories.

12. "National Art" is another name for "gung fu."

13. Hawkins Cheung was one of Yip Man's senior Wing Chun students, who trained at Yip Man's *kwoon* in Hong Kong while Bruce Lee was training there in the 1950s.

14. The name of the recipient of this letter is unknown. This first draft was found in one of Bruce Lee's earliest notebooks from Seattle, written while he was completing his high school requirements.

15. "Dianne" was evidently one of Bruce's classmates at Edison Technical School.

16. Ed Hart was Bruce Lee's second private student in Seattle. The letters to Hart were written by Lee while Hart was in New York for several months.

17. Jesse Glover was Bruce Lee's first student in America.

18. The Tso family and Bruce Lee's family were close friends when Bruce lived in Hong Kong during the 1950s, and they remained friends throughout his life. Mrs. Tso, Pearl's mother, was like a second mother to him, and he often sought her advice. In fact, he wrote her frequently to inform her of his progress in America. The two friends exchanged letters and postcards, some of which were brief and aphoristic, while others, such as the letter reprinted here, were much more soulful and in-depth.

19. "Linda" is Linda Emery, who would become Bruce Lee's wife on August 17, 1964. This letter was written just five days before their first "official" date, which, as she recalls, took place on October 25, 1963.

Dear Fred,   April 9 1966

It might be a surprise but instead of writing you from Hong Kong, I am writing from Los Angeles. You see, "Batman" is such a hit (though I kind of think it silly) that the "Green Hornet" is sold without a pilot and script! In other word, the series will definitely be out this coming season, which is this coming September. At present 20th Century Fox is sending me to drama school----the drama coach is Jeff Corey, the best here in Hollywood----- at $70 an hour (if I were to pay I'll tell them I've got it!). The lessons (three times a week) is doing me a lot of good and make me more fluid with not-acting acting -----a most difficult way to achieve, unnatural naturalness. At any rate, we are to start shooting on the 23rd of May.

I'll be playing Kato (doesn't sound like a Chinaman, does it), the right hand man of the Green Hornet. Instead of carring all kinds of weapons, this fellow is to Gung Fu all his opponents--------------

At present, besides taking acting lessons I'm giving private lesson in Gung Fu (actually will start the end of this month). Among my prospective students are Steve McQueen, Paul Newman, Vic Damone, Tommy Sands.......... It won't be bad. At least I'll be having pocket money(at $25 an hour) till the shooting two months away. It will be a lot of fun and this job will take care of raising a family. Financially wise this job is most satisfying.

When you are free do drop me a line and let me know how things are going on with you. Please give my best regards to Amy. Your girls have grown quite a bit, especially the younger one.

Take care my friend-------I better stop. You see my typing is kind of slow like "seek and ye shall find"

Part 2

FROM GUNG FU TO GREEN HORNET

(1964–1966)

1964

To Taky Kimura[1]*

Process in Learning Gung Fu

★ Self-cultivation

The point where to rest being known, the object of pursuit is then determined; and, that being determined, a calm unperturbedness may be attained too. To that calmness there will succeed a tranquil repose. In that repose there may be careful deliberation, and that deliberation will be followed by the attainment of the desired end.

Wishing to cultivate oneself, one first rectifies his heart (mind).

Wishing to rectify his heart, one seeks to be sincere in his thoughts.

Wishing to be sincere in his thoughts, one first extends to the utmost of his knowledge—such extension of knowledge lies in the investigation of things.

Remark: It cannot be when the root is neglected, that what should spring from it will be well ordered.

A rectified mind is a mind immune to emotional influ-ences—free from fear, anger, sorrow, anxiety, and even fond at-tachment—when the mind is not present, we look and do not see; we hear and do not understand; we eat and do not know the taste of what we eat.

Not allowing outside things to entangle this mind; in other words, outward changes do not move the mind. Its function lies in suppression of the senses, and on reduction of desire.

A gung fu man rests therein, and because he rests, he is at peace. Because he is at peace, he is quiet. One who is at peace and is

*Notes for Part 2 begin on page 81.

quiet, no sorrow or harm can enter; therefore his inner power remains whole and his spirit intact.

—The nature of water is that if nothing is mixed with it, it remains clear; if nothing ruffles it, it remains smooth.

Definition:
1. To be one thing and not to change, is the climax of STILLNESS.
2. To have nothing in one that resists, is the climax of EMPTINESS.
3. To remain detached from all outside things is the climax of FINENESS.
4. To have in oneself no contraries, is the climax of PURITY.

"NO MIND"   "NO THOUGHT"

Discard all thoughts of reward, all hopes of praise and fears of blame, all awareness of one's bodily self. And, finally closing the avenues of sense perception and let the spirit out, as it will.

The highest skill operates on an unconscious level.

Sincere thought means thought of concentration (quiet awareness). The thought of a distracted mind cannot be sincere. Man's mind and his behavior are one, his inner thought and outer expression cannot contradict each other. Therefore a man should set up his right principle and this right mind (principle) will influence his action.

If you look within yourself and are sure that

Bruce Lee with Taky Kimura (left) and Charlie Woo (right)

you have done right, what do you have to fear or worry about? You require only to perform your own mission in life without any thoughts of aggressiveness or competition. Follow the will of nature and coordinate your mind and your will to become one with nature, and nature will protect you.

Yielding

Yielding will overcome anything superior to itself; its strength is boundless.

The yielding will has a reposeful ease, soft as downy feathers —a quietude, a shrinking from action, an appearance of inability to do (the heart is humble, but the work is forceful).

One should be in harmony with, and not rebellion against, the strength of the opponent. Such art will "preserve ourselves" by following the natural bends of things.

Placidly free from anxiety one acts in harmony with the opponent's strength. One does not move ahead but responds to the fitting influence.

Nothing in the world is more yielding and softer than water; yet it penetrates the hardest. Insubstantial, it enters where no room is. It is so fine that it is impossible to grasp a handful of it; strike it, yet it does not suffer hurt; stab it, and it is not wounded.

★ Law of Non-Interfering

One should be in harmony with, and not rebellion against, the strength of the opponent. Such art will "preserve ourselves" by following the natural bends of things; consequently, we achieve immortality because we do not wear ourselves out. This theory is illustrated in Taoism, [in the story] about the perfect butcher whose carving knife remains perpetually sharp because it always goes between the bones and tissues and never meets any resistance.

To Rest in Weakness Is Strength

"Alive, a man is supple, soft; in death, unbending rigor. All creatures, grass and trees, alive are plastic, but are pliant, too, and [in] death all feeble and dry. Unbending rigor is the mate of death, and yielding softness, [the] company of life. Unbending soldiers get no victories; the stiffest tree is readiest for the ax. The strong and mighty belong to the bottom, the soft and yielding rise above them all.

The strongest is he that makes use of his opponent's strength—be the bamboo tree which bends toward the wind; and when the wind ceases, it springs back stronger than before.

To Bill Evans[2]

Posted from Oakland, California, on September 2, 1964

Dear Bill,

I am sorry to inform you that the articles have to be delayed because I am at present on a tour demonstrating gung fu.

I've just got back from Los Angeles not too long ago and I'll have to start again in San Francisco. In a week or so I'll have to fly to New York.

However, I'll try to find time in between to finish the articles. By the way, there should be a coverage of the last tournament at Long Beach, and when will the next *Black Belt* be out?

For your information the symbol in the seal of the Jun Fan Gung Fu Institute is the symbol of Yin and Yang in which the Yin & Yang (black [passive] & white [active]) are two interlocking halves of one WHOLE, each containing within its confines the qualities of its complementaries (not opposite!). Instead of [being] mutually exclusive, they are mutually dependent and are a function each of the other.

When I say "the heat makes me perspire," the heat and per-spiring are just "one" process as they are co-existent and one could not exist but for the other. Just as an object needs a subject, the person in attack is not taking an independent position but is acting as an assistant. After all, you need your opponent to complete the other half of a whole.

Thus gentleness/firmness is one inseparable force of one unceasing interplay of movement. If a person riding a bicycle wishes to go somewhere, he cannot pump on both the pedals at the same time or not pump on them at all. In order to move forward he has to pump on one pedal and release the other. So the movement of going forward requires this "oneness" of pumping and releasing, and vice versa, each being the cause of the other.

This "oneness" is just a basic idea in the symbol. Then there is moderation without going to either extreme, the wonder of the or-dinary. . . . In general, however, the idea is that—if gung fu is extra-ordinary, it is because of the fact that it is nothing at all special—it is simply the direct expression of one's feeling with the minimum of lines and energy. The closer to the true Way, the less wastage of ex-pression there is.

Please pardon my incoherence and poor penmanship.
Bruce Lee

To William Cheung, Hughes, A.C.T., Australia[3]

Posted from Oakland, California, on October 30, 1964, at 9:00 PM

October 30, 1964

Dear William,
Our correspondence has always been like this: a mountain stream—it meets and parts. Anyway, I'm writing again after not too long an absence, considering the previous length of time.

It has been a year since I'm back from Hong Kong,[4] and as you have noticed on this letter cover that I've moved from Seattle to Oakland, California. It has been a few months now that I'm here and things are coming along pretty good. At the present time, I'm taking courses from the University of California. By the way, I'll be getting a degree in philosophy.

Actually how are you getting along? I've met a few fellows while I was back in Hong Kong and according to the different reports I've heard I really don't know what to think. Also, I saw the twin brothers (one of them) while walking along the Hong Kong street. Are they back to Australia? I heard they are rather obnoxious. Hawkins Cheung is in Hong Kong now.

Nowadays I indulge myself in reading and gung fu practice. I'm staying with a fellow who is also a nut in the Chinese art (this guy is really practicing—he can break a bottom brick without breaking the first one),[5] and together we practice two hours a day.

We have a nice gym built in the garage and my wooden dummy is set up. My partner has also built two other different dummies that prove to be of much use to Wing Chun form and method. We are in the process of completing some protective equipment for actual sparring without pulling punches.

Hope to hear from you soon,
Bruce

To William Cheung, Hughes, A.C.T., Australia

Posted from Oakland, California, on November 22, 1964, at 9:00 AM

Nov. 21, 1964

Dear William,
Your letter is kind of stressing doubt on our friendship. I don't wish to write to have you think that I'm writing for Gung Fu informa-

tion—I'm writing merely because I want to write to you. Please do not stress on the need (as you mentioned in your letter) on my part for your opinion. Of course you helped me while we were in Hong Kong and I'm grateful, but please write to me as a friend, not as one who has all the answers, which I'm sure no one has. These are facts I'm putting down and am not trying to be disagreeable.

Things are getting pretty good here in Calif. and if I have not told you that I'm married, well, I am—she is a real nice girl and is a straight 'A' student. We have been married for a year something now. In fact, we are going to have a baby soon.

Just as an object needs a subject, the person in attack is not taking an independent position but is acting as an assistant. . . . You need your opponent to complete the other half of a whole. . . . Thus gentleness/firmness is one inseparable force of one unceasing interplay of movement.

The book you read is a basic book I've written somewhere in 1963[6] and I'm in the process of completing a much [more] thorough book on the Tao of Gung Fu.[7] It will be the size of Nishiyama's book [*Karate: The Art of Empty Hand*] if you've seen it. This book will contain my insight during these past five years, I've worked hard for it.

My wife and I are planning to take a trip to Hong Kong next year, that is if I can make it. It will be nice if you can go too. I bet it would be difficult to get off a government job for a few months. If you can make it over to the States do let me know ahead of time, I'm sure we can put you up in my house.

Truly yours,
Bruce

1965

To Taky Kimura

The following announcement card was posted on February 1, 1965, the day that Brandon Bruce Lee was born.

February 1, 1965
Our Baby's here.
Name: Brandon B. Lee
Date: Feb. 1, 1965
Weight: Eight lbs., eleven oz.
Parents: Mr. & Mrs. Bruce Lee
A big healthy boy of course!

Brandon Bruce Lee—July 1965

To Taky Kimura

February 1965

Taky,
When I mailed my letter today, I received your letter. Thank you for the income tax form and what not. You know, if you were a Chinaman I would think you are trying to be funny by ending the letter, "Your See Hing" [Your Senior], Taky. . . .[8]

    Well, I guess I wouldn't be in *Life* magazine yet because they want to concentrate first on "Batman." You better take damn good care of yourself and don't move too much yet, and let Chris take care of the class. You have to push. . . to help push gung fu in Seattle.

    [The martial artist you mentioned] is no sweat as he doesn't even understand what is rhythm (timing) & distance, which is the core of all martial art. Of course simplicity is a necessary component, too. When he does open the class, I do not think he will be a threat as I know you have better basic requirements, though he is "blown up" with so-called muscles, [they are] not efficient ones, unfortunately.

I'll see to it that the dummy will be on the way, even if I have to send it myself. I didn't give that demonstration on the 20th of this month because I am not in the mood for it—I might help Ralph Castro on his World Tournament this coming 6th of March.

I have stopped training for two weeks now and will resume again when I'm back in Hong Kong. On this trip I'll pick up more flowery [gung fu] forms and what not for the TV show—the viewers like fancy stuff anyway.

The first chance I have I'll film the Wing Chun 3 Forms[9] and tai-chi and whatever I feel that will be helpful and beneficial to you. It will be in 8 mm.

My mind is made up to start a system of my own—I mean a system of totality, embracing all but yet guided with simplicity. It will concentrate on the root of things[10]—rhythm, timing, distance—and embrace the five ways of attack.[11] This is by far the most effective method I've ever encountered or will encounter. Anything beyond this has to be super-fantastic. Wing Chun is the starting point, chi sao is the nucleus, and [they are] supplemented by the FIVE WAYS. The whole system will concentrate on irregular rhythm and how to disturb and intercept the opponent's rhythm the fastest and most efficient way. Above all, this system is not confined to straight line or curved line, but is content to stand in the middle of the circle without attachment. This way one can meet any lines without being familiar with them. Wait till I assemble everything.

Lately, I've been working on my book and it is nearly finished except for more photo taking.

Enclosed find some pictures I happened to run into when I looked for my stuff. Old Charles is in it. . . .[12]

Linda sends her regards. Brandon is growing and growing.

Take care and do not over-exercise yet.

Bruce

P.S. By the way, did you say you lost your membership card?

Letters of the Dragon

To His Wife, Linda[13]

Posted from Kowloon, Hong Kong, February 16, 1965, at noon

February 15, 1965

Linda,

I'm most comforted to receive your letter, especially at a time like this. The whole family is in a state of sadness and confusion.

The burial took place yesterday at 4 PM and tomorrow we'll go visit the tomb. The service was a cross between Chinese custom and Catholic regulation; the whole deal was one mess of conflict, which I'll tell you when I see you.

As for my return I cannot yet give you a definite date because I have to wait for the lawyer to clear the whole matter. All in all, I'll do my best to come back as soon as I can. You do not have to worry about me as I'll take care of myself and use my better judgment.

One thing I'm anxious [about] is your health and secondly my son, Brandon. I hope you will go have a check up and bring Brandon boy along, too. Never mind about expense, your health is more important. Any amount you need will be okay with me. If you're short of cash get it from mother and I'll reimburse whatever the amount.

According to the Chinese custom I'm not supposed to go visit any friend, have any hair cut or shave, wear any gold watch or ring... all in all I look like a pirate with long hair and whiskers.

By the time this letter reaches you I might have given you a phone call already—I do not know yet because all money and property are tied up until the reading of the will. Peter Jones Wong will fly to Vancouver and I'll get in touch with him and have him call you. I hope to get hold of him before he leaves H.K.

In the meantime you must take good care of yourself and Brandon. Do not forget to go to the doctor and above all do not forget to let me know of the result (like your blood count, etc.). If there is anything that has to be done, do it! (like Brandon's shots, or anything) Do not worry about expenses. I'll be able to pay for it.

Take good care of yourself and Brandon boy.

With all my love,

Bruce

P.S. Find out the circumference of your head plus hat size for wig.

To Linda

Posted from Kowloon, Hong Kong, on February 17, 1965, at 8:00 AM

Linda,

The family is now calming down a lot, but there are as yet a lot of things to be done.

Tomorrow we will have to go to the lawyer to obtain the will, and according to the lawyer the will cannot be settled till after six

Bruce Lee with his mother, Grace Lee (right) and long-time family friend Eva Tso (left)—Hong Kong, ca. 1963

months. Right now I'm trying to finish all necessary official documents on my part. You know, we will have to pay eighteen thousand dollars for legacy tax!

Most likely I am coming back somewhere [around] March 8 in as much as I like to be with you and Brandon. I'll be flying in to Seattle and to-gether we'll fly back to Oakland. I'll get in touch with you ahead of time to let you know of my arrival. By the way, give me your phone number in your next letter.

This trip I'll devote my time with Mrs. Tso as she is very

lonely. I have to because I've left all my friends' phone numbers at home. Together with Mrs. Tso I'll try to pick up some clothes for you. Give me the sizes of coat (top) etc., etc. I have that card you wrote down but still give me once more the necessary information.

Today, after many days of strain and stress, I've finally gone to the bath house where I've enjoyed a comfortable day of bathing and massaging. Tonight a famous movie star is coming to my house; the two of us will go out, have something to eat and chat. He's a nice guy.

Due to the fact that there was not too much ready cash in the safe (and we can't touch anything in the bank before the will is cleared) we do not have enough to make a call to you. Most likely they cannot forward me back the money (traveling expense) until six months from now.

When I come back you'll be happy with some of the stuffs I bought you. By the way, can you cut a little bit of hair and, together with the measurement of your head and hat size, send it to me?

Take very good care my dearest.

Love,

Bruce

To Linda

Posted from Kowloon, Hong Kong, on February 21, 1965, at 4:00 PM

Feb. 21, 1965

Linda,

Today is Sunday and I'm writing this letter at the house of Mrs. Tso. Tomorrow we'll go to the telephone company to make a long distance call to you. Mrs. Tso will call Pearl.

How's my son Brandon? Next time write and let me know

how he has changed into.

I wish you were here now instead of next year. Wait till you come here. Boy, I'm sure you will flip—definitely. Also, you do not have to worry how to act; everything will flow.

Tomorrow we'll go shopping. I'll pick up a diamond ring for you.[14] As for clothes I think it is wise for you to come personally and pick up whatever you wish. We'll stop by and have [our] honeymoon in Hawaii, Japan and, of course, Hong Kong. Baby, this trip you'll remember the rest of your life. I can promise you that!

To hell with the gym.

To Linda

Posted from Kowloon, Hong Kong on February 22, 1965, at noon

February 22, 1965

Linda,

Although the date has not [been] officially set up but I'm planning to leave on the 6th of March, eleven more days from today.

It's Monday today and I've received two of your letters, one dated on the 17th, the other on the 18th. It seems you or rather Seattle is rather behind on all my letters—I mean it takes a long time to get there. At any rate I'll call you either tomorrow or day after tomorrow.

The reason I can't call today is because Auntie Mary's husband Mr. Tse has arranged a special showing of some gung fu films from China. This is a golden opportunity and he might be able to reduce them from 33mm to 8mm so I can buy them.

Tomorrow I'll go out with Mrs. Tso again to try and make that phone call to you—I hope it will go through. You know, I'm really looking forward very much to the coming Hong Kong trip when you, Brandon and I will have one hell of a time. If Feb. we can't make it we'll make it whenever we can. Come high, come low we've got to go—damn the torpedo, full speed ahead!

When I come back there won't be any clothes as I've said that it isn't practical when you aren't here; however, you [can] be sure there will be some goodies. On the next trip you can buy to your heart's content.

With love always,

Bruce

PS: Say, how's the look of Brandon boy?

To Linda

Posted from Kowloon, Hong Kong on February 26, 1965, at noon

Feb. 25, 1965

Linda,

Received your letters today.

I'm most happy to have talked to you and hearing your voice was very comforting. Before I forget, my flight number is 624Y, Western Airlines, and I'll

Linda and Bruce Lee

be arriving at 10:07 PM at Seattle. I planned to stay for around a week and see how things are. By the way, [I'm flying back on] the 6th of March, Friday night.

I'm very glad to hear of Brandon's progress. I can't wait seeing him again—not to mention you of course. You know, I always picture walking with you on a Hong Kong street. It'll be cool. Man! I really can't wait for this coming trip.

From Gung Fu to Green Hornet (1964–1966)

Inform Taky, Lanston, Charles, etc., etc., of my returning and till then I'll meet you.

With all my love always,

Bruce

P.S. Do not forget to make last minute check to find if plane is on time—if I'm on that special plane, etc.

To Linda

Posted from Kowloon, Hong Kong, on February 27, 1965, at 4:00 PM

Feb. 26, 1965

Linda,

Eight more days and I'll be in Seattle. Man, sometimes I wish I'd never made this trip.

I think I've lost weight; how much I've lost I'm not sure, but I can tell from the smallness of my face—you know me, it's always in the face.

Yes, I believe you should exercise more often in the future; right now, just take care of your health. According to your letters, Brandon boy must be pretty fat—I mean the way he eats.

Wait for the future trip to come—we'll buy the whole [of] Hong Kong. Be prepared for it. I know you'll enjoy this honeymoon trip.

I have a purse for your mother and if financial situation allows I might be able to pick up more stuffs for her. I'll try but you know the U.S. Customs, not to mention money problems. I'll use my judgment.

Today I'll go to the hair-dresser with your measurement plus hair. I hope to pick up a wig for you. They are not too expensive—considering it is real human hair. It runs around H.K. $350 to $450—around half the price of what they charge in U.S.

I have to wrap up some books for shipment now. Take very good care of yourself—see you in around a week.

Love,
Bruce

To Linda

Posted from Kowloon, Hong Kong, on February 27, 1965, at 4:00 PM

February 26, 1965

Linda,
It's 9:20 PM and Mrs. Tso has just left my house. Today I went with her to the hair-dresser and ordered a wig for you; it runs about $US 90. I asked the hair-dresser to set it; later on you can have it set any style you want. The hair-dresser is now trying to find some hair to match your color.

Also, I bought you a diamond ring. I won't describe it now and wait till you see it personally. I picked up James' jade earrings when I was at the jewelers. When I pick up the diamond ring tomorrow I'll try to get a gift for your mother, too.

Well, it will be Saturday tomorrow, a week from the 6th, the date of my departure. I'll leave on the 6th and also arrive in the States on the 6th—a day difference, because Hong Kong is one day ahead. So I'll see you on the 6th [in the] evening in Seattle. We'll stay for around a week.

I've picked up two more Cantonese self-taught booklets for you. You'd better practice because we'll be in Hong Kong in a year's time. We'll stop in Japan and Hawaii on our way back. We have to! It's our honeymoon, you know.

By the way, part of your birthday gift is included in the gifts that I'll bring back from Hong Kong. They will be all placed securely; let's hope the customs officials are blind.

Tomorrow I have to go for the fitting of my three suits plus a top coat—not to mention my two new pants. Man, they are slick, but not as slick as the stuffs I'm going to bring back to you. Let's hope I'll bring them through without the customs official finding out. I can't afford to pay tax on them all. In fact, I'm broke starting tomorrow. You'll know why when you see me: wig, ring, etc., etc., etc. . . .

Good night my dear wife,
Bruce

To Linda

Posted from Kowloon, Hong Kong, on March 1, 1965, at 3:00 PM

Feb. 29, 1965

Linda,
Received both your letters of Feb. 23 and Feb. 25. It's Monday in Hong Kong.

James wrote and [it] seems like everything is in bad shape; of course, he might just be over-exaggerating a little bit. By the way, Dickie is using the Plymouth everyday to [go to] work now and James said that we might have to buy another one.[15] At any rate, I'll discuss things with you when I see you in Seattle, which is, according to my time (a day ahead of yours), five days from now.

I don't think James got Bo Bo out yet.[16] Let's hope we can straighten things out when we get there. Also, write down the money we owe your mother, like doctor visits, etc., etc. I'll have everything squared away.

Peter will most likely be staying in Hong Kong—at least a year anyway. He is planning to teach school here. As for Agnes, she is leaving on the 8th, I believe.

Langston wrote me a letter and expressed his sympathy. Peter

Jones was here and is now in Japan; he should be back in around 2 or 3 days. By the way, he will move and stay in Vancouver as of early April.

You know, I wish I were in Seattle right now or maybe you were here in Hong Kong. It's pretty boring. I'm writing this letter in bed and that's why the penmanship is so loused up—can't compare to my everyday penmanship. Did I tell you I have the best hand-writing? Well, anyway. . . .

It's tiring like heck to write in bed and at the same time this letter is running out of space, so baby, I'll be seeing you in 5 days. By the way, no need to wake Brandon up to [go to] the airport. I'll see him at the house. Tell me, is he better looking now? Of course, I couldn't tell exactly. Well, I'll wait for the picture.

Love,
Bruce

To Linda

Posted from Kowloon, Hong Kong, on March 3, 1965, at noon

March 3, 1965

Linda,
Received your letter of Feb. 27

Strangely enough, March 6 happens to be also Saturday here in Hong Kong (I've just checked the U.S. calendar—it's also Saturday). At any rate, as far as I know, and it is written down on my plane ticket, that I'll leave on the 6th of March and arrive in San Francisco also on the same date, the 6th of March at nine something PM at night.

Immediately an hour later I'll then take Western Airlines and fly to Seattle, arriving at 10:07 PM. The flight number is 624y. This is the correct information up to date; however, I will call you long distance when I arrive at SF airport.

Too bad the color pictures didn't turn out—we'll have to find a better camera for Brandon boy.

It's the third today, three more days of [waiting before] my departure. I can't wait to be home again. I have a lot of things to talk to you [about].

I hope this letter will arrive on time—which I doubt very much. At any rate, I'll send it and we'll see. I'll call you at SF airport to be sure.

This afternoon I'm going to have tea with a producer, Mr. Tse, the husband of Auntie Mary. After that I'll be going to Mrs. Tso's house. I've been to her house every day since my arrival in Hong Kong.

Well, like I said, I've a lot to tell you and discuss with you.

Till then, my dearest wife.

With love from,

"China James Bond"

To Taky Kimura

Posted from Kowloon, Hong Kong, on May 10, 1965

Dear Taky,

Here I am, writing once more from Hong Kong. Linda and I have been here for around three days now and she likes every bit of it, except the growing heat. She never had it so good—you know, servants and what not.

I plan to stay here for around three months and, as soon as 20th Century Fox writes me I have to go back to the Hollywood studio for either some more tests or the pilot. As you've probably known I've signed a contract with the agent, Belasco, who, by the way, is also agent for Nick Adams and many others.

Keep me informed on the club and if you send anything to me, the place to send it is my Hong Kong address.

By the way, is there anything I can pick up for you in Hong Kong? Don't hesitate to ask.

I'll keep you informed of my trip.

Take care and have fun,

Bruce

To Taky Kimura

Posted from Kowloon, Hong Kong, on May 30, 1965

May 28, 1965

Taky,

I've been showing Linda around and that's why I've not written till now.

Linda enjoys every bit of it—except the hot weather (not as bad as 1963)—she has also bought quite a few tailor-made clothes.

I'll be here till 20th Century Fox notifies me to return for the actual shooting, which will be another two more months I think. Although a contract has been proposed, the whole deal is not 100%, however, it is 70% that it will succeed. At least that's what my agent told me.

In the meantime I've been teaching my brothers and some friends gung fu at my house. They are very enthused over the whole deal. I, too, am working on my transformation of simplicity to yet another more free-flowing movements of no limit limitation.

Oyama's book *This Is Karate* is out and it is quite interesting as it contains quite a few of [the] ancient gung fu methods.[17] As for actual application of techniques, it is still too far behind. He admits that gung fu's theory is more sound and practical.

Shocked to hear of the 2nd Clay-Liston fight. If it wasn't a fix, Liston must have timed in on the on-coming force of Clay's punch.

By the way, if there is any dues I'll appreciate it if you can send them to me.

Also, do report on the class['s] progress as well as yours and Charles['s].

Bruce

To Taky Kimura

Posted from Kowloon, Hong Kong, on June 8, 1965, at 6:00 PM

June 7, 1965

Taky,

Thank you for your letter plus money order. I, too, was surprised at the outcome of the Clay/Liston fight; I can only say this, Liston must have timed his rushing in with the right hand punch of Clay so well that even he (Liston) was knocked out cold—that is if nothing else was involved in the fight.

You are right that Liston is slow when he comes to chase a fighter, but Clay is yet to be proved against other fast moving fighters. You know, it is the style of Clay that screwed up Liston the most.

So Mr. "I don't think so" met the same fate as Masafusa and got himself deported. Too damn bad for him, aside from all obnoxious manners, he is quite a likeable fellow—sometimes.

[The fellow you mentioned] is an extremely lazy fellow but he does like to show off a little bit, so I am kind of amazed that he will find time (from not sleeping or gambling) to B.S. the Chinese bunch in Chinatown. As far as skill or basic requirements [are] concerned, you [have been] ahead of him for quite some time. In fact, knowing him, [although] he might be talking this or that, he is scared of you inside. This is no kidding. Show him a little respect and this sucker is dying to show you all his fancy movements. If you have time, you might learn a few forms (set up by him from books probably) from him. It is useless for me to tell you the techniques aren't worth a damn, but you will find out. Since we met, his style has changed.

Charles bought a house! What the hell [does] he want with it? [Maybe he'll] get married or something.

I'll find out about the wooden dummy the first chance I get; I think the dummy will help you in sharpening your skill.

Talking about method, my style has [now been] formed, but [I'll] have to see you personally to explain [it].[18] The idea can be summed up as this—just as it is difficult to come in on an opponent with no *bai-jong* (thus, no guided lines or boundary) it is more difficult to [find a solution for] a method with no exact style or method (yet governed by an immovable FIRST PRINCIPLE).[19] TIMING and DISTANCE are the basic stuffs, but Wing Chun principle is the nucleus (the most important foundation).

By the way, Robert Wise will contact me regarding a part in the movie "Sand Pebbles."[20]

B.

To James Yimm Lee[21]

Posted from Kowloon, Hong Kong, on July 30, 1965, at 8:00 AM

July 29, 1965

James,

James Yimm Lee (left) and Bruce Lee, ca. 1969

Your letter arrived one hour ago. Thank you for your ideas on [the wooden] dummy and the ordering of those books.

Before I go on to show you the counter offensive of the techniques you ask, I'll go on with this letter first. I'm going to use another air letter for the illustration of *sil lum tao*.

By the way, we've finished the shooting of the whole set of sil lum tao and many other [techniques], demonstrated by my sifu Yip Man. Over 130 photos have been taken and when we're through there will be way over 200. These pictures will prove to be valuable when my book comes out as never before [has] the Wing Chun master, sifu Yip Man ever been on photograph. He is 66 now, I think, and years after that these photos will be the only set.

Nice to hear Johnny Choy is coming—too damn bad you can't make it.

The bai-jong makes sense but other than that all techniques are not so cool. This old man Leung has asthma and is pretty sick lately and that's why he can't continue to show me other styles. If time permits I hope to get as many other chop sueys as possible to formulate my style, which I've been working on nearly every day as I've nothing else to do.[22] You know how "Master Lee" is living now!

Good to hear about your not [the] selling teak wood [furniture] to Bob. I plan to buy them back on my return. Buddy, forget about the additional $200. You don't have to pay me.

Here are some counters for that technique that got you perplexed. It can be countered during its formation, at the finish, or after its formation.

Note: Chinese characters accompanying Bruce's sketches: (panel A —"slap hit"), (panel B —"disengage to shovel hook"), (panel C —"left straight punch" / "into lop sao (pulling hand)" / "with left elbow sinking down")

Letters of the Dragon

To James Yimm Lee

Posted from Kowloon, Hong Kong, on August 1, 1965, at 8:00 AM

July 31, 1965

James,

In my formation of a more complete Wing Chun I've added on an INDIRECT PROGRESSIVE ATTACK to the original *chi sao*, which is close quarter combat. Indirect Progressive Attack is the link to achieve chi sao.

Indirect Progressive Attack is used against an opponent whose self-defense is tight and fast enough to deal with Simple Attacks like Straight Blast, Finger Jab, and Trapping Hit. . . .

Indirect Progressive Attack (I.P.A. from now on) is based on feinting, and feinting is to DRAW the opponent to the execution of a parry or block. REMEMBER that although feinting consists mainly of 2 movements (sometimes three, but no more than that!) they must be ONE smooth flowing action. The following notes will help you to understand the execution of feinting, which will make you advance into your opponent's defense faster and safer.

A) The First Movement (feint) must be long and deep (by that I mean penetrating) to draw the parry. The second real movement (attack) must be fast & decisive allowing the defender no possibility of recovery—long-short—even in the delivery of attack with two feints, the depth of the first feint must force the opponent to move to the defense—long-short-short.

B) Gain Distance—to shorten the distance the hand had to travel by a good half with your feint, and leave to your second movement only the second half of the distance—known as Progressive Attack.

C) Gain Time—(by deceiving the parry so that even [though] you are slower, you can still strike him). To time this movement of arm crossing from left to right (right to left, up to down, down to up), for the execution of the direction to that of the attack [i.e., to move in the same direction as the force of your opponent's attack]—it is while the opponent's arm is traveling across that he must start his offensive action—thus the second movement (in other words, the attack after the first movement which is the feint) should move ahead of the opponent's parry, that is being deceived by your first movement, the feint.

I hope after much thinking on the above note you will begin to feel this Indirect Progressive Attack. Remember that speed must be regulated to coincide with the opponent's movement.

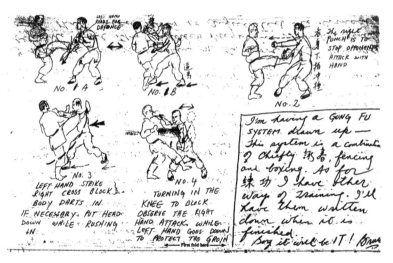

Note: Chinese characters accompanying Bruce's sketches: (No. 1B—"Horse stance"), (No. 2—"move your body by side-stepping to the right, while performing a low block and then go immediately to a straight punch")

I'm having a gung fu system drawn up—this system is a combination of chiefly Wing Chun, fencing and boxing. As for training,

I have other ways of training. I'll have them written down when it is finished.

Boy it will be IT!

Bruce

To James Yimm Lee

Posted from Kowloon, Hong Kong, on August 7, 1965, at 4:00 PM

Aug. 6, 1965

Jimmy,

The following is a suggested gung fu training program for the class instruction:

I. Limbering Exercises—a "must" in the general program to strengthen and to limber (flexibility) main parts of the body are:

1. Waist—Twisting, bending (front, back, left & right), and rotating.
2. Leg—Mainly stretching or kicking (front kick & side kick).
3. Shoulder—Rotation & pulling back stretch.
4. Arm—Mainly push-up or any basic weight training you think beneficial.
5. Wrist—Rotating, flexing, or with weight.

Use your own ideas based on creating new ways to improve the function of the body in gung fu—the hell with conventional methods and opinions.

II. Punching—Paper, partner facing, sandbag, etc.

III. Kicking—Partner facing.

IV. Techniques—As used before or any sensible move you can choose.

Make use of the wooden dummy and equipment available at our "Shaolin Temple" gym. It will be a challenge to you to CREATE ways and means to better the training method—use karate, judo, aikido or any style to build your counter-offensive from.

It will be interesting!

Bruce

To James Yimm Lee

Posted from Kowloon, Hong Kong, on August 8, 1965, at 8:00 PM

August 7, 1965

James,

Glad to have received your letter and hear that you're training hard by yourself and [with] Jimmy Ong.

This is the usual counter on that foot hook (actually, by your measured distance, he shouldn't be able to come close in without being hit by a punch or practically anything. . . .

(Horse Twisting)

elbow him (with left) while leading him back

right foot advance

Note: Chinese characters accompanying Lee's sketches: (left—"shovel hook"), (middle—"horse twisting"), (right—"turning horse stance and straight punch")

In regards to the 73-year-old master from Formosa being the reason for the "runner" not opening a gung fu school [it] is a lot of bull.[23] First of all, is this old master a nut? I mean does he go around closing up gung fu schools? If he does and if he is really, really good at his age, then the B.S. artists will be the first victims. There is a saying, "live and let live," so the "runner's" not opening a gung fu school has nothing to do with this old man. After all, a man at 73 can't afford to go around using physical violence, maybe verbal violence.

As for the "runner's" gung fu school, it's just another waste of time with a little bit more to offer—calisthenics! The more I think of him to have fought me without getting blasted bad, the more I'm pissed off! If I just took my time, [but] anger screwed me up—that bum is nothing!

Bruce

To James Yimm Lee

Posted from Kowloon, Hong Kong, on August 13, 1965, at 10:00 PM

August 13, 1965

James,

To damn bad for Dicky—he should know better than not to pay parking tickets! They always say in Chinese, the officials (officers) have two mouths and they can charge you with anything.

Glad to hear you're practicing sil lum tao and am especially happy to hear you understand that sil lum tao is all the ways of the Wing Chun Hand in a nutshell. For better results in sil lum tao I advocate iron rings on forearms while doing "open hand" and "close hand" as the weight gives the actual resistance of the opponents.

Instead of pure imagination, a real feeling is being felt on arms as they slowly go outward from the body (MAIN POINT—fingers and wrist relaxed!!!). I've shown the iron rings method (I've made 8, 3 pounds each) to my instructor and he is convinced when I demonstrated to him that in sil lum tao when the "open hand" is coming out it is supposed to be going into a "close hand" and when a "close hand" is coming out it is supposed to stop the oncoming "open hand." Thus, the iron rings will give the necessary resistance when the practitioner directs his energy outward without tensing his fingers and wrist. More resistance can be provided by wearing more iron rings. This is an alive way of building "long bridge force" without getting the hands rigid. This is a kind of modernized pro-gressive weight training method that is effective. Anything for the betterment of Wing Chun.

No, I do not have the pleasure of bumping into [the runner] or [the other man you mentioned]. Aren't they supposed to have returned already? As for the "founding the bridge" and "finger jab," it will be easier to teach you when I see you on my return.

As of today, I haven't yet received the protein but I'm sure it should arrive tomorrow or a day after. How much has it cost you? Say, do I have a stack of magazines in the closet? It's all right if they are not there, I must have packed them.

Take care of yourself, old boy

Bruce

To James Yimm Lee

Posted from Kowloon, Hong Kong, on August 17, 1965, at 8:00 PM

August 16, 1965

James,

Received your first airogramme letter. It was wise to use them when nothing is enclosed in; it is definitely much cheaper.

Your elbow strike is good, but must be done after or at the same time [as] the block (by right shoulder and left hand) and not in horse stance as 50% weight in the front leg while opponent's powerful sweep is in, is dangerous. More weight should be back to

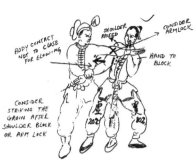

Note: Chinese characters written on legs of righthand character: (right leg—"light"), (left leg—"heavy")

the rear. The right raised shoulder is also important to lead opponent off-balance toward his front for elbow strike (maybe even an armlock can be applied without wasting motion—experiment).

Your description of [the] qualifications of certain students is right. Thus, knowing this you yourself should build around their lacking—improve your power/speed, flexibility (general) and mental attitude (confidence, killing instinct, . . .). NO MATTER WHAT STYLE SUCH BASIC REQUIREMENTS ARE NECESSARY!

The fellow you mentioned is a nice guy basically—try not to fool around too much half-heartedly in front of him. If you move, move your best as though not really trying. This sucker likes to criticize this and that. This goes [for] all onlookers.

Let me know if you've worked out the dummy design as I've not yet made one—if it can be improved on, let me know.

Good luck on the Japanese laundry lady—well, who knows! She might even support you and you can spend your time on traveling and gung fu. Glad to hear [about] your good training program for students.

By the way, how's Dicky after that jam?

Brandon is getting bigger—that guy's got the basic requirement and the killing instinct—he is screaming now!

So long. Ah boy, got to look after the "little sifu."

Take care,

Bruce

To George Lee[24]

December 18, 1965

George,

It was nice to see you when I was down in Oakland.

I must thank you once more for the grip machine (not to mention the dip bar, the name plate and others...). When you make something it's always professional-like.

My gripping power and forearms have improved greatly—thanks for your wrist roller.

Linda and I will be coming down to Oakland to stay for around a month before either going to Hollywood or Hong Kong. The 20th Century Fox deal is 85%. If that doesn't come out I have two contracts waiting in Hong Kong.

During this coming one month stay I want you to drop by at least once a week at the house. Because I want to show you all the gung fu techniques. I know you will benefit greatly from these instructions and I trust you will not show it to other students.

I'm drawing the following diagram to show you [what] a naval head-guard looks like:

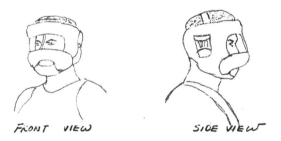

FRONT VIEW   SIDE VIEW

The protective equipment is the most important invention in gung fu. It will raise the standard of gung fu to unbelievable heights. In order for gung fu to remain supreme over the other systems, the protective equipment is a must. With the ability you have in making things, I have confidence in your building the first practical protective equipment in the history of gung fu. Your work will be remembered. Gung fu NEEDS it.[25]

I've written to James to tell him to help you in every way he can. If you need any help call him. Start with this great plan at your earliest convenience and devote whatever time you have. This plan depends on YOU because knowing the rest of the guys, they do not have the incentive or the ability.

Take care of yourself my friend,

Bruce Lee

The grip machine George Lee constructed based on the design Bruce Lee provided.

1966

To George Lee

March 31, 1966

Dear George,
Just a letter to see how my favorite student is coming along—

Postcard, ca. 1966, showing Van Williams and Bruce Lee in and out of costume for their roles as the Green Hornet and Kato.

I'm sorry that I couldn't teach you as we planned because there is a slight change in the 20th Century Fox deal. Probably James Lee has told you about it; at any rate, "The Green Hornet" is going to be on the air this coming September.

At present I'm taking acting lessons from [the] very well known Jeff Corey, the best drama coach here in Hollywood.

I'll be giving private lessons before the series starts. The prospective students are so far Steve McQueen, Paul Newman, James Garner, Don Gordon, and Vic Damone. The fee will be around $25 an hour.

Understand that you are going to start with James again. It's nice [to hear this] and you should stick with it and go as often as you can. Keep asking questions and follow what I've told you that night.

I'm developing fully The 5 Ways of Attacking and even James

doesn't know it. Next time when I see you I hope I'll have time to show you and teach you because George, you've got what it takes and your attitude certainly deserves the best.

"The Green Hornet" will start shooting at the end of May and I'll be busy like hell but the first chance I have, I'd like to take a trip to Oakland and we should go out to dinner.

Take care my friend and drop me a line when you have time. By the way, unless you know him well, do not give my address to [any of] the students.

Thanks,

Bruce

To Fred Sato[26]

April 9, 1966

Dear Fred,

It might be a surprise but instead of writing you from Hong Kong, I am writing from Los Angeles. You see, "Batman" is such a hit (though I kind of think it silly) that "The Green Hornet" is sold without a pilot and script! In other words, the series will definitely be out this coming season, which is this coming September.

At present 20th Century Fox is sending me to drama school—the drama coach is Jeff Corey, the best here in Hollywood—at $70 an hour (if I were to pay, I'll tell them I've got it!*). The lessons (three times a week) [are] doing me a lot of good and [are making me] more fluid with not-acting acting—a most difficult way to achieve unnatural naturalness. At any rate, we are to start shooting on the 23rd of May.

---

*That is, if Bruce were to have to pay for the lessons personally, he would tell them he had mastered it already in order to avoid paying what was then a very high fee.

I'll be playing Kato (doesn't sound like a Chinaman, does it), the right hand man of the Green Hornet. Instead of carrying all kinds of weapons, this fellow is to gung fu all his opponents. . . .

At present, besides taking acting lessons, I'm giving private lessons in gung fu (actually will start the end of this month). Among my prospective students are Steve McQueen, Paul Newman, Vic Damone, Tommy Sands. . . .

It won't be bad. At least I'll be having pocket money (at $25 an hour) till the shooting two months away. It will be a lot of fun and this job will take care of raising a family. Financially wise, this job is most satisfying.

When you are free, do drop me a line and let me know how things are going with you. Please give my best regards to Amy. Your girls have grown quite a bit, especially the youngest one.

Take care my friend—I better stop. You see my typing is kind of slow, like "seek and ye shall find."

Bruce

To Taky Kimura

April 18, 1966

Taky,

It's nice to have received your letter. Everything is running smoothly here in L.A. If I didn't tell you, the date has [been] set for the shooting (though as of now there isn't a Green Hornet);[27] it will be on the 23rd of next month.

By the way, I'll be moving to another really "cool" apartment, the Barrington Plaza—a 27 stories high luxury tower with doormen and attendant parking, laundry & dry cleaning valet service, Olympic-size pool, all-wool carpeting, all electric kitchen (dishwasher, built-in range and oven, etc.), electronic huge elevators—

I'll be living on the 23rd storey (the higher, the more expensive) and I'm telling you it's something else.

However, do not think for a moment that I'll pay $300 a month for this apartment (that's how much it actually costs); you see the half owner of the apartment wishes to take gung fu from me and so I got a damn good deal on it. The present apartment I'm living in costs $120 (L.A.'s apartments cost more—especially in the western part) and get a load of this—for those fancy deal (oh, there is a beautiful breakfast bar, too) this apartment that I'm moving in now costs me $140 a month! All the services I mentioned—like doormen, attendant parking, security guards, house services—are all included in the deal.

By the way, Batman and Robin also live there.[28] So for two hours [of] private lesson for the owner, I only pay for half the rent. This Barrington Plaza is a famous spot here and you have to see it to appreciate it—like a park inside with two gigantic 27 storey tower buildings surrounding it, with all kinds of stores and what not on the bottom level. They claim you can live a year inside the place without having to go out and buy anything!

So much for that. I'm glad to hear that the boys are loyal to the school. I think Chris should be promoted to 3rd. His loyalty certainly demands attention, but his laziness and [lack of] drive is something else—well, I'll leave this matter in your hands and you will have to judge and see what fits. You are the head instructor in charge and you will decide on him—on the rest of the boys, in fact. You have the authority to give out rank, you know. By the way, you are the only one that can do so. So let me know what your decision is and if there is any membership card that needs to be stamped by my seal just tell the student to send them to you and you mail them to me.

Let me tell you an incident that is a warning to us all. The Japan America Society of Southern California was presenting a demonstration of "The Defensive Arts—Aikido, Judo, Kendo, and Karate." H.N. was heading the demonstration and I and the ex-publisher of *Black Belt*, Ed Jung was there. It was a disappointment! The H.N. of four years ago (in Washington) has slipped and what [there] is now is an old man—like he couldn't even snap decently, nor can he show his techniques smartly—not even in a classical manner. It was a quick change from the last time I saw him. At least at that time he could classically demonstrate his techniques with precision and snap—so that goes to prove the old Chinese saying "Song (singing) never leave the mouth, fist never leave the hand." Do we have to work, work, work—the aikido is something else! Completely out of reality. There might be a strong aikido man, but his power is evidenced only when he practices among his fellow partners who will dance with him and fool around with his flow of ki.[29]

Taky, you have something over [that other martial artist you mentioned]—that is not being classically inclined and the ability to express yourself explosively and economically. The more I observe the prevalent karate men here [in the West], the more I'm amazed at the public that ignorantly eats up such [an] impractical mess [without] at least analyzing karate with their [own] more alive [and] certainly more practical sport [of] boxing! If you want to excel in gung fu, you have to throw away all classical junk and face combat in its suchness, which is simple and direct. Forms and classical techniques that [the martial artist you mentioned] teaches are "organized despair" that serve only to distort and cramp his students and distract them from the actual reality of combat. Such means of practice (a form of paralysis) solidify and condition what was once free and fluid. Throw away mysticism and B.S., it is really nothing but a blind devotion to the systematic uselessness of practicing routines and stunts that lead to nowhere.

Even a man that moves classically fast and snappy is really not too much to be praised—you see he is trying to set a rhythm, not to adjust [to] broken rhythm, which is the thing that will happen in actual combat. Then you have to take reactional speed, etc., etc., into consideration. Most of the self-defense systems are "dead" because the classical techniques are futile attempts to "arrest" and "fix" the ever-changing movement in combat and to dissect and analyze them like a corpse. When you come down to it, real combat is not fixed and is definitely very much "alive."

I've been busy like hell with acting lessons and gung fu lessons (the same stuff I teach in the group class—nothing spectacular) and tonight I'm invited to attend an Academy Award dinner party in Hollywood. Nick Adams (a black belt, supposedly), Sal Mineo, etc., will be there.

If you want to excel in gung fu, you have to throw away all classical junk and face combat in its suchness, which is simple and direct.

I'll shoot the techniques and what not as soon as I can find time. I might fly to Vegas this week to meet Sinatra—nothing definite yet.

Good luck on the Japanese girls' class. Use creativeness in the girls' class and think in terms of their likes, without messing up the central theme. I'll mail selling pointers when I find the time.

Take care my dear friend,

Bruce

To Fred Sato

May 4, 1966

Dear Fred,

Thank you for your last letter that reached me at my present address which you will find on the top of the envelope. I've moved to this new apartment the 20th of last month.

So you are teaching at the University of Washington—how do you like it? Do you have to cram in a lot of 'throws' in a short period of time?

By the way, what does this Mr. Lee Cameron want? I haven't received a letter from him yet. I'm kind of curious as to what he wants, do you know? Taky didn't get in touch with me either.

The show is re-scheduled to be shot on the 1st of June, and the first premier show is on the 9th of September. Right now I'm busy like heck for interviews and publicity pictures, etc., etc. I might be flying in to New York for a press interview in a week or two. *Movie Screen* magazine will come to our apartment and do a story on [us] this Friday.

It is most interesting to work on the coordination of arm and body for that will make a judoka able to exert twice (perhaps triple) his power and a gung fu man to strike his bodyweight. Using arm force alone is indeed characteristic of the untrained person (in fact, a lot of instructors are practitioners of this) and since striking is mainly used in gung fu, I'll discuss the relationship of arm power and body power (waist or hip movement) in a punch. I'm sure that there will be a similar basic source as in throwing.

It will facilitate the analysis of putting in the waist with the arm by dividing the human body into two halves with an imaginary center line as in Fig. 1.

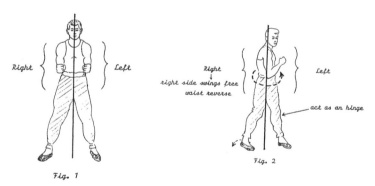

Fig. 2 shows a person releasing his right side and propelling his bodyweight (as in an ordinary right hand punch) by bracing himself on his left foot that acts as the hinge around which his right side bodyweight and power rotates. The hip and shoulder are driven first to the imaginary center line then the arm comes into play 'explosively.' The whole idea is to transfer the weight to the opponent's target area before the weight transfers to the left leg. That is also why in stepping in to strike, the leading foot should not land first, or the bodyweight will rest upon the floor instead of being behind the striking hand. Of course, all these are coordinated very, very fast; but the waist reverse does come a split second faster.

If you manipulate this imaginary center line it might evolve some new angle for your judo analysis. From this center line I was able to construct a nucleus and later on able to jump away from the nucleus and establish out of line and broken rhythm counter attack. Thus

My theory that states—1) learn the center, 2) keep the center, and 3) dissolve the center... can be stated more generally—1) learn the rules, 2) keep to the rules, and 3) dissolve the rules.

my theory that states—1) learn the center, 2) keep the center, and 3) dissolve the center. Or it can be stated more generally—1) learn the rules, 2) keep to the rules, and 3) dissolve the rules.

By the way, emphasis must be made to the students to throw with their body because of the fact that in terms of force and power, the arms have but one quarter of the force of the body when set in motion. Secondly, the movements of the waist are long and free while those of the arms are short. You can say that one turning of a large axis is equivalent to many turnings of a small axis.

I definitely agree with you that the arms do exert maximum strength toward the end of the movement—therefore, the arms are the vehicle of force that is released by the body through this center line idea. Boxing also makes use of this center line business but expresses it in too big a motion. It is all right at first but later on it should be guided by the principle of simplicity—to express the utmost in the minimum of movements and energy. However, in terms of judo, the movements can be a little more than gung fu because it doesn't involve striking and counter-striking.

If I were to work on judo I'd make use of this centerline (I haven't really worked on it—on top of that I have limited knowledge of the subject) and classify the attacks in judo something like:

1. Direct Attack—quick and powerful one action drive in to throw opponent.

2. Combination Attack—To combine two or three throws in a row to disturb the opponent's rhythm.

3. Indirect Attack—To use false attack to draw a reaction from the opponent and make use of this reaction for your throw— seems like this field is rarely used in Oriental systems. Everything starts from immobile to mobile. Feints and what not, if done in a threatening manner, can disturb even a calm and cool operator.

4. Attack by Drawing—Apparent opening to opponent and counter his attack to it.

There are more than that I'm sure, but in order to build on it, one has to jump out from the classical rigidity and see the field in a more practical light—as weight training (not bodybuilding) has contributed to judo.

I can go on and on but unfortunately I have to go for a luncheon interview with my publicity man. It's always nice to have such discussion with you, and whenever you are free do drop me a line and we will continue where we left off. In this summer if you have time you should get together with Taky and exchange ideas with him. I'm sure you will find it interesting.

My best to Amy and the kids—have you seen any good samurai movies? Watch for a blind swordsman movie, it's great.

Take good care and have fun with your work.

Bruce

P.S. Will you please find out for me regarding this Mr. Lee Cameron—without the Cameron I would have taken him for my countryman.

To George Lee

George,
I heard from James that you didn't feel good. I hope you are much better by now.
Take care my friend,
Bruce

To William Dozier[30]

June 21, 1966

Dear Mr. Dozier,
Simplicity—to express the utmost in the minimum of lines and energy—is the goal of gung fu, and acting is not too much different.

Since the first episode [of "The Green Hornet"], I've gained actual experience. I've learned to be "simply human" without unnecessary striving. I believe in Kato and am truthfully justifying the physical action economically.

Actually, what I [would] like to express here is regarding the relationship between the Green Hornet and Kato. True that Kato is a house boy of Britt, but as the crime fighter, Kato is an "active partner" of the Green Hornet and not a "mute follower."[31]

Jeff Corey agrees, and I myself feel that at least an occasional dialogue would certainly make me "feel" more at home with the fellow players. It does take a real pro to just stand there in big close-ups. I've learned the effectiveness of simplicity, but in order to cultivate simplicity, something to say or do is necessary—from firmness comes gentleness, and complexity leads to simplicity. However, alone standing there apart from the fellow players listening, is itself simplicity stripped to the very end. That requires considerable skill because it is simple!

I've presented two ["Green Hornet"] scripts to Jeff Corey, but so far we've been doing other exercises because there just isn't anything in the script to work on.

I'm not complaining, but I feel that an "active partnership" with the Green Hornet will definitely bring out a more effective and efficient Kato. My aim is for the betterment of the show and I bother you with this because you [have] been most understanding.

Thank you very much.

Sincerely,

Bruce Lee

To Vicki[32]

Dear Vicki,

The art I use on TV is not karate. It is the ancestor of karate and is known as gung fu, which is of Chinese origin (so is karate).

Breaking boards and bricks are mere stunts and are not recommendable for anyone, especially a girl like you. Techniques are the main goal you should work at. If you want to break something, use a hammer.

Thank you for writing. I enjoyed your letter very much.

Bruce

To George Lee

June 25, 1966

Dear George,

It was nice of you to call.

I'll probably come down one weekend in the middle of next month to pick up some of the weights. By the way, the grip machine you made for me is darn good, and it helps me in my training very much.

From left to right: George Lee, Allen Joe, Bruce Lee, and James Yimm Lee

If and when I make the trip, I will let you know, as I [would] like to get together with you.

Thanks again for your thoughtful call, and do drop me a line when you have the time.

Take care my friend,

Bruce

To Taky Kimura

November 6, 1966

Taky,

A letter to let you know that "The Preying Mantis" episode [of "The Green Hornet"] will be on the 18th of Nov., which is two weeks from this Friday (we're pre-empted because of a special). Also, a week after that "The Hunter & The Hunted," an episode in which I do gung fu without the mask.

The show is doing bad, rating wise. Dozier is trying to make it go by changing it into an hour show. Whether or not we can change it remains to be seen. For our sake, we better.

Next week I'm doing a pictorial layout of gung fu in color in the Dodger Stadium for *TV Guide*. You know, whether or not this show will go, the show will last at least till March. So gung fu will have enough exposure and so [will] Kato, Bruce Lee.

The schools will definitely go. I'll discuss with you in more detail. I'm preparing for it. Let's make use of this opportunity, buddy.

Take care,

Bruce

P.S. Let Fred Sato and different friends know of this coming episode, "The Preying Mantis."

Notes

1. Taky Kimura was one of Bruce Lee's dearest friends and also one of his first students. In fact, Bruce Lee thought so highly of Taky's abilities and character that he made him assistant instructor at his Seattle school. He sent Taky the following cards, containing what he considered essential points in the "process in learning gung fu," which focus on the philosophical or "higher" aspects of the art, rather than on the purely combative.
2. Bill Evans was an editor at *Black Belt* magazine in the early 1960s.
3. Like Bruce Lee, William Cheung was a student of Yip Man. He was also Bruce's childhood friend.
4. Bruce had returned to Hong Kong in the summer of 1963 with one of his gung fu students, Doug Palmer.
5. The "fellow" is Bruce's student, James Yimm Lee. Immediately after they were married, Bruce and Linda moved in with him and lived with him for several months. James was the assistant instructor at Bruce's Jun Fan Gung Fu Institute in Oakland, California.
6. The book Bruce Lee is referring to is *Chinese Gung Fu: The Philosophical Art of Self-Defense*, which was self-published in 1963. (It has been reissued by Ohara Publications, Santa Clarita, California.)
7. Bruce Lee's *The Tao of Gung Fu* is volume two in the Bruce Lee Library series (Boston: Charles E. Tuttle Co., 1997).
8. Even today, Taky Kimura laughs:

> I thought that I could impress Bruce if I signed off the letter in Chinese. I'm of Japanese persuasion myself, so I didn't know that much Chinese. For some reason though, I got *See-hing* (your senior, one who learned before you) confused with *See-dai* (your junior, one who learned after you). Fortunately, Bruce had a good sense of humor about it, and realized that I wasn't trying to be a smart-aleck, but simply got my terms mixed up—I had a hard time living this one down, though.

9. The three forms of Wing Chun are sil lim tao ("little imagination"), chum kiu ("searching for the bridge"), and biu gee ("flying fingers").
10. Bruce Lee sought the "ultimate" connecting principle, or the "root" that connected all efficient martial techniques (and later on all spiritual truths) throughout development of his martial art, and the evolution and expression of jeet kune do. (See also *Jeet Kune Do: Bruce Lee's Commentaries on the Martial Way*, volume three in the Bruce Lee Library, pp. 385–86.)
11. The "Five Ways of Attack" are: simple angle attack (SAA), attack by drawing (ABD), attack by combination (ABC), progressive indirect attack (PIA), and hand- or hair-immobilization attack (HIA). This last attack also included immobilization attacks on the legs or leg-immobilization attacks (LIA). (See also *Jeet Kune Do: Bruce Lee's Commentaries on the Martial Way*, volume three in the Bruce Lee Library, pp. 103–25.)

12. "Old Charles" is Charlie Woo, a friend and student of Bruce's from his early years in Seattle. Charlie died at a tragically early age from injuries resulting from a horseback riding accident.

13. On February 8, 1965, Bruce Lee's father, Lee Hoi Chuen, passed away in Hong Kong. Bruce was summoned for the funeral service and penned the following letters home to his wife, Linda, during his stay in Hong Kong.

14. As Linda and Bruce could not afford "real" wedding rings when they were married, he had promised to pick up a real diamond ring as soon as possible.

15. "Dickie" was James Yimm Lee's stepson.

16. "Bo Bo" was the name of James Yimm Lee's dog, a boxer. Later, Bruce and Linda had a Great Dane named Bo, who proved to be a very high-maintenance animal.

17. Mas Oyama, the famed Japanese karate master.

18. Bruce was already teaching his nonclassical gung fu out of the Jun Fan Gung Fu Institute. The "style" that he created while he was back in Hong Kong was "the Jun Fan method." In 1967, he would officially rechristen it jeet kune do (the way of the intercepting fist) and, shortly thereafter, come to disbelieve in the notion of styles or schools of martial art altogether, which he considered to be divisive and obstructional to an individual's search for truth in martial art. For this reason, he closed all of his martial art schools in January 1970.

19. The by-jong is the ready stance or ready position in gung fu. Bruce initially used the term to refer to the classical combative stance of Wing Chun. He later dropped this stance in favor of the more fluid on-guard position of jeet kune do.

20. *The Sand Pebbles* was a movie starring Bruce's future student Steve McQueen. Bruce did not get the part (presumably the supporting role of the male Asian boxer), which went instead to the Japanese-American actor, Mako.

21. James Yimm Lee was one of Bruce Lee's closest friends and a very capable martial artist in his own right.

22. "Chop suey" was Bruce's joking name for the type of martial artist who was determined to create something new simply by combining random components of all sorts of Chinese gung fu styles, without paying proper attention to the principles of simplicity, directness, and efficiency. (See also *The Tao of Gung Fu,* volume two of the Bruce Lee Library, page 166.)

23. The "runner" was the name that Bruce Lee gave to a Chinese martial artist who, along with three other Chinese martial artists, showed up at his kwoon one day in 1964 and delivered an ultimatum: Either stop teaching non-Chinese the art of gung fu, or accept a challenge to fight. Lee accepted the challenge but, as soon as the fight began, the challenger actually turned and ran away. Bruce Lee chased him all around the kwoon, finally caught up with him, and forced him into submission. However, Lee felt tremendously winded from all the running and this led him to reformulate his views of martial art. It proved to be the genesis of his personal art, jeet kune do.

24. George Lee was one of Bruce Lee's earliest students as well as a very close friend. He also happened to be one of the most talented craftsmen whom Bruce Lee ever met. The two forged a close friendship and George built most of Bruce Lee's training equipment and artistic representations of his martial and philosophical beliefs.

25. It is important to note that Bruce Lee's ideas and innovations concerning adding "realism" to combat training gave birth to the notion of reality-oriented martial art schools, and even to sports such as "full contact karate."

26. Fred Sato was a judo man and a friend of Bruce's from Seattle.

27. Greenway Productions, the company that produced "The Green Hornet" TV series, had signed Bruce to play Kato several weeks prior to signing Van Williams to play the Green Hornet.

28. Batman and Robin were played by Adam West and Burt Ward, respectively.

29. *Ki* is Japanese for the Chinese term *chi,* or "inner energy."

30. William Dozier was the producer of "The Green Hornet" television series.

31. Britt Reid was the Green Hornet's alter-ego in the TV series.

32. Vicki was evidently a young fan of "The Green Hornet," which premiered on September 9, 1966, and ran until July 14, 1967. Vicki had written to ask Bruce whether the martial art that Kato used was karate and what was the best way to break a brick with her hand.

Twentieth Century-Fox Television, Inc.

BOX 900
BEVERLY HILLS, CALIFORNIA

George,

I've been shooting Batman these few days and busy like hell. I believe I should be able to find time to show your boy and his friends around the studio this coming Friday.

The Oklahoma appearance was great and I'm asked back for another one in Georgia. That sign you made has created quite a hit — everyone admires your talent.

If you have time, I like to make two requests for some stuffs that you can make for me. They are gadgets to put my system across.

First, I like three signs ~~like~~ for hanging like picture on wall ~~in posters~~ — slightly smaller than the sign you made for me. Here are the plans & ideas — this project by the way is to illustrate the thought behind my system — the 3 stages

1.

PARTIALITY
THE RUNNING TO EXTREME

2.

FLUIDITY
THE TWO HALVES OF ONE WHOLE

3.
EMPTINESS
THE FORMLESS FORM

Part 3

JEET KUNE DO AND THE ART OF CULTIVATING OPTIMISM

(1967–1970)

1967

To George Lee

Tuesday, January 31, 1967

George,

I've been shooting "Batman" these [past] few days and [have been] busy like hell. I believe I should be able to find time to show your boy and his friends around the studio this coming Friday.

The Oklahoma appearance was great and I'm asked back for another one in Georgia.

That sign you made has created quite a hit—everyone admires your talent. If you have time, I'd like to make two requests for some stuffs that you can make for me. They are gadgets to put my system across.

First, I [would] like three signs for hanging, like pictures on a wall—slightly smaller than the sign you made for me. Here are the plans & ideas—this project by the way is to illustrate the thought behind my system—the 3 Stages.

Explanation for the Three Signs
(same black shining background as the sign you made)
First Sign

Here all we need is one red half and one gold half of the Yin Yang symbol. HOWEVER no dot is needed on either half; in other word, it is just plain red with no gold dot, or just plain gold with no red dot (this serves to illustrate extreme softness or/and extreme hardness). So just follow the drawing and also put the phrase—PARTIALITY—THE RUNNING TO EXTREME on the black board.

Second Sign

Exact Yin Yang symbol like the sign you made for me except there is no Chinese characters around the symbol. Of course, the phrase—FLUIDITY—THE TWO HALVES OF ONE WHOLE will be on the black board.

Third Sign

Just a shiny black board with nothing on it except the phrase EMPTINESS—THE FORMLESS FORM.

The three signs have to be the same size because they illustrate the three stages of cultivation. Please do make them like the sign you made for me; aluminum symbol and shiny black board.

The second gadget I have in mind is used to dramatize the not too alive way of the classical so called kung fu styles. What I have in mind is a miniature "tombstone" and here is the drawing:

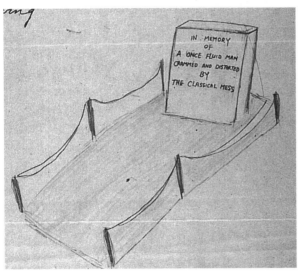

Miniature "tombstone" made by George Lee based on Bruce Lee's drawing (left).

I'm sure you know how a grave looks like and make it with any material you like (aluminum tombstone is fine) and at any size you want. Not too small though, because it's for display.

Call me collect if you have any problem.

Thank you in anticipation,

Bruce

To George Lee

Dear George,

Masterful! Simply masterful! Dan and Linda are stunned when they see the Yin/Yang symbol. Like I said previously, it is very artful.[1]*

Also, I must thank you for the name plates and the stainless steel card container—they are the greatest! My deep appreciation for your time and thoughtfulness.

First of all, I like you to mail me your membership card at your earliest convenience.

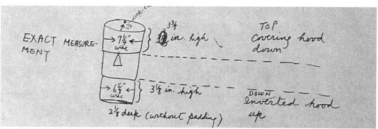

The drawing on the bottom of [the] first page gives the exact measurement. In comparison to a human head, the width 7 1/4" is from ear to ear, the height of 3 3/8" is from forehead to top of nose, and the deepness of 1 1/2" is from front of head to back of head. Now to the bottom part, the neck, as on a human. The height, 3 1/8" is from underchin to bottom of neck above collar bone, the width 6 5/8" is from the end of neck to the other, and the deepness of 2 1/8" is from throat to the back of neck.

All the above measurements are made without padding, in other words, the exact measurement on the equipment. Another thing I like to point out is that for the top, the hood is covering over the head; however, for the bottom, the hood has to cover the neck inverted; in other words, bottom up.

Thank you once more for everything.

Thank you ever so much,

Bruce

---

*Notes for Part 3 begin on page 137.

To George Lee

Dear George,

Too bad you aren't here. You should have heard [the] comments from the fellows down here! "Is he a pro artist?" "I don't believe this!" (Dan said that) and many, many more on the fine work you've created.

As for me, they are terrific!!

Thanks once more for the many hours you've put in; you're the greatest.

Bruce

To George Lee

April 26, 1967

Dear George,

I'll be going to New York on the 1st of May, then to Washington, DC for an appearance. After that I'll go to Seattle for two days and will stop by Oakland for a day before returning home.

It will probably be on May 10 that I'll stop by Oakland, at that time let's get together and have a gung fu session.

The latest is that Greenway Productions will most likely pick up my contract—a one hour series is in the planning.[2]

Take care,

Bruce

To George Lee

May 1967

George,

I am coming to Oakland on May 26, this coming Friday at around 5 PM and will go to James' Fremont class for a short lecture-type lesson for his students. Then I would like to get together with you, James and Allen for a gung fu session (probably next day, Sat.).

However, if you can go to the Fremont class with us you can come and leave your car at James'. I think you do know some of the students there.

At any rate, hope to see you this trip, and that nothing sudden comes up to prevent me from coming.

Take care,

Bruce

To George Lee

June 1967

George,

I'm coming to Oakland this coming Monday night around 9:30 PM. I'll probably give you a call.

I'll stay till Thursday afternoon and then will take off to New York for an appearance at the All American Open Karate Championship. I'll stay there for four days then I'll go to Seattle for a few days and then will come back to Oakland for a few days before I'll take off for Springfield, Mass. for another appearance.

Plan on coming down for the photo-shooting on the weekend of July 8.[3]

Will talk to you when I see you,

Bruce

To His Wife, Linda[4]

Posted from Inglewood, California, on June 15, 1967

Linda,

Well, it's one hell of a struggle, a long steady walk with spoon in steady hand, but I did give her the cod liver oil. She ate good yesterday (Wednesday).

Today she just ate once (it's 4 PM now) and getting the tape off her ears I accidentally cut her ear, a slight one, not bad. Will attempt to catch her off guard from behind to administer the cod-liver oil today.

Well, I won't be back to Oakland to pick Bo up till July 5 because Belasco called to let me know that there is a $750 offer to go to Springfield, Mass. for a one day performance (3 times in one day) and I'll leave LA on July 3 (Monday night) and will probably return either July 4 night or July 5. Maybe I'll have James send Bo back, instead of going back to pick her up. I don't know yet, I haven't decided.

Ted Wong brought over oyster sauce beef last night and stayed over till around 12. There was a "kung fu" demonstration on "Johnny Carson."

Will go over [to] the shopping center for dinner because boxing's on tonight. Will go to Bo's doctor tomorrow morning at around nine AM.

The kids keep coming over—it's a bore. So I'm not going to answer the door anymore; I'll just peep through the side window.

Yesterday I drove the car to the field and let Bo run for a while—I ran with her and walked fast around the field a few times. Will go again today and drop this letter by the mail-box on my way there.

Take good care.

Love,

Bruce

To Linda

Posted from Inglewood, California, on June 16, 1967

Linda,

Just returned from Bo's doc—left at 10:30 instead of 9:30 AM, couldn't make it—and received your letter plus those photos we made. Only two of the group look half-way decent; my hair was kind of long. I'll bring them up with me and will phone them to let them know I couldn't return in 7 days.

Anyway, I got Bo's tranquilizer pills and they are to be taken two at a time, two hours before departure.

Henry Cho called last night and he is sending tickets this week (tomorrow I should receive them). I'll leave for Oakland Monday night and will leave there on Thursday afternoon (June 22). In New York I'll stay till the 27th and will leave that Tuesday morning.

I'll straighten the dog food delivery before departure—hope to receive information from you that I asked [for] in [a] previous letter regarding whether or not they will have [made the] delivery this coming Tuesday. At any rate, I'll have the whole matter straightened up before I leave.

The remaining one pear in the can has long [since] been gone into my stomach. The cheese is slowly decreasing as I use them in Bo's meals.

I'll keep Bo with me till I leave from Oakland. That means I have to go buy some dog food for her for that three days there. Every morning Bo comes up to the bed and lays close to me. I'm sleeping on your side and she is sleeping on the edge. One morning I didn't get up till 11 and she just slept there. Of course, I got up at around eight to open that back door.

I haven't been eating lunch as I eat a late breakfast, a big bowl of Familia with protein, etc. etc. During the afternoon I might just eat a high protein bar. However I haven't been losing weight.

Out with Bo everyday, I drive her to the field instead and run around there. Haven't been doing the rest of [the] exercises, but still keeping up with the stomach exercises.

It's 12:27 PM Friday noon and I'll bring this letter to the post-office and pick up a bottle of papaya juice. Have to sneak out quietly, Bo is sleeping in her bed.

Bruce with the Lees' Great Dane, Bo.

Love,

Bruce

To Linda

Posted from Inglewood, California, on July 3, 1967

Linda,

Arrived safely with the house in good order, and Bo is sleeping on the big bed now. Called Susan and she will take Bo.

One thing will be screwy is the fact that my plane takes off at 9 tomorrow morning and I have to go pick up the ticket at the post-office, which will open at 8:30 AM!

Bought milk and some canned dog food plus some ready to eat food.

James, George and Al will be coming Saturday morning.

Agnes has moved—a big guy broke into her apartment with only she and her baby there and she saw him come in, so she closed herself in the bedroom and called the next door neighbor. That sucker is a chicken and dared not to come in, so he left and went for the police. In the meantime, Bing came back (the big guy heard the baby's voice and ran out) and Bing began to knock on the bedroom door without calling, so Agnes was yelling all over the place thinking it was the big guy—so anyway, I left word to have Agnes write you to let you know whether or not she can come pick you up.

Let me know if Agnes can come pick you up. If not, I'll get someone else. By the way, Agnes air-mailed the camera to Seattle. When I went to her house, I got stuck to help moving.

Will write you another letter upon arrival on Wed.

Take care my dear wife,

Bruce

To Linda

July 3, 1967

Linda,

Am on the airplane heading for New York—left Bo at Susan's with food and all, got everything straightened out and nearly missed the plane due to Dan's punctuality (called taxi, but paid service charge and left with Dan instead).

There was some mail (mostly ads and bank statement, magazines, etc.) including the one you sent from Seattle. It was transferred from Oakland to first address on Wilshire, then to Barrington Plaza, then to Inglewood. I guess from now on without the c/o James Lee will follow this same procedure.

WILL CONTINUE LETTER UPON ARRIVAL AT NEW YORK AIRPORT.

Here I am inside American Airlines airport waiting—an hour and a half more to go. I phoned Kenneth Kwong in New York, but it's rush hour and I can't possibly make it to his restaurant and come back on time for the flight to Agawam, Mass. He asked me to stop by before returning to LA. I told him I might if I do stay an extra day in New York. I'll have to call Susan to let her know. I doubt that I'll stay though, as I'm sick of traveling around. By the way, two persons stopped me for autographs and pictures (taken with them) when I was inside the airport.

WILL CONTINUE UPON ARRIVAL AT HOTEL TO-NIGHT.

It's 11:30 PM and I'm at a motel in Agawam, Mass. [There was] a full page ad of me in the newspaper which I've included in [with] this letter. By the way, I won't be stopping by New York, and, dig this, Gene, Belasco's associate called, and I'm having an interview at Universal studios on July 5 (Wed. for a good part in "Ironside" starring Raymond Burr). So I feel pretty good about this as this might lead to something nice faster.

I'll let you know after my interview (probably I'll call you).

Good night, my dearest wife and I love you.

Say hello to your mom and everybody.

Love,

Bruce

To Linda

July 5, 1967

Linda,

Just called you on the phone and I'm sure you're glad to hear of the success of my interview. Though it's only $750 for 3 days work, I hope it will open some doors after that. It was nice to hear your voice.

Bo has been eating regularly again—for a while her schedule is all messed up—and Fred really digs her and tells us that if we have to go anywhere just to leave her.

I haven't been out with her because when she came back from Oakland I've noticed a big sore on her right toe and when I went out once with her the other day before leaving for Agawam, the sore reopened a little bit. It's much better right now, but still tender. So I'll wait a little till it's completely healed before trying the rough ground. By the way, most of the grass is burnt away in that field.

On your way back just stay maybe an afternoon at Agnes' new house in Alameda and as long as your presence there is fulfilled, I'm sure it's all right.

Unless you wanted to stay, in that case let me know and make arrangements for a late flight like coming back at around 9:30 PM or 8:30 PM, so I have time when I return from Universal studios. I don't know but I'm sure you too are tired of traveling.

It was peace-like when I returned to 2509 W-115th Pl. and it will be home-like when you and Brandon are here. I miss you both.

Take care and drive carefully coming back to Seattle.

Love,

Bruce

To George Lee

July 1967

George,

It was nice seeing you in Oakland and thanks again for that "beautiful" stand and "cool" pins you made for me. Ted Wong thinks you are the greatest craftsman.[5]

The two handles you made for the finger bowl do not fit as the four holes on the side of the bowl do not match the screws on the handles.[6] I imagine it's rather difficult when the bowl is already here in LA. Enclosed are the positions of the four holes on each side of the finger bowl.

When you can find time (any time from now) do drop me a line so that I can send you a plane ticket to come down during a weekend. I'm sure I can sharpen your gung fu techniques during this period. Of course at the same time you can look over my desk.

I'll be working on my book once again now that I'm settled down and those photos you were in look great.[7]

Take care my friend.

With appreciation,

Bruce

To George Lee

Letter posted September 5, 1967

September 5, 1967

George,

Finally moved but still unpacking and a lot of rearranging. It's a hell of a job but I must take time out to once more thank you for that magnificent job you did on that finger jab equipment.

I've already heard from James that the base for the leg stretcher will be terrific. Actually I need not have him to inform me on that. Man, like everything you touch has to be beautiful or else you won't deliver it.

I'm flying up this weekend, give me a call at James' and we'll get together. I will sharpen at least one of your techniques with my newly found training method.

Okay, George. Take care my friend,

Bruce

To Taky Kimura[8]

Taky,

I've just rushed the tai kik wall chart form to you. Enclosed in the parcel was a Chinese jacket.

As I've mentioned, I've just got back from Oakland and James Lee is going to send you a lop sao apparatus with built-in resistance.

First and foremost, I like to impress a most important rule of teaching in your mind, and that is the economy of form. Follow this rule and you will NEVER feel like you have to ADD more and more so-called "sizzling" techniques to keep our students interested.

In order to explain "Economy of Form," I'll take a technique to illustrate the theory. Later on, this idea can be applied to any technique. Together with the idea of "The Three Stages Of A Technique" [1. synchronization of self, 2. synchronization with opponent, 3. under fighting condition] this program of teaching not only provides an endless routine of instruction, but a most efficient lesson plan that will bring results to ALL students. I've tested them here in LA and disregard how LITTLE we show each time, the students' interest is kept up because they have to eliminate the extra motions involved, and they feel great doing it. All right, back to the idea of "ECONOMY OF FORM."

To illustrate the idea, I'll take the pak sao (slapping hand)— basically, "ECONOMY OF MOTION" means ALL motions start from the by-jong position; secondly, HANDS ARE TO MOVE FIRST IF IT IS A HAND TECHNIQUE [FOOT FOLLOWS], FEET FIRST IF IT IS A FOOT TECHNIQUE.

So, emphasize the above "Two Truths" by practicing pak sao first in the touching hand manner—in other words, students in bai-jong position touching each other's hand—though in real combat, one will never start by touching hand, however, this touching hand position will ensure correct form in the beginning stage—economy of form, that is.

Each student must attack [in unison] FROM THE BAI-JONG without any wasted motion. Now this has been an overlooked basic theory of utmost importance. If any student does his pak sao [or any technique for that matter] with wasted motion, back to the touching hand position he goes to MINIMIZE his unnecessary motions. So you see that in order to progress to apply pak sao from a distance, this touching hand position has to be mastered.

Not only that, the student has to return to the touching hand position to remind him to eliminate unnecessary motion periodically.

From a distance, pak sao is a lot harder—without any given away motion, one must initiate first hand, then feet, in a progressive, harmonious forward motion—no wonder not too many can hit with a single pak sao! Do you not see now the idea of economy of motion? Just this  *A most important rule of teaching… is the economy of form. Follow this rule and you will NEVER feel like you have to ADD more and more so-called "sizzling" techniques to keep our students interested.* one theory of economy of motion takes up one heck of a lot of time for perfection, not to mention the "Three Stages Of A Technique"—that is, in terms of pak sao, after learning and mastering pak sao from a distance, one has to bridge the gap between [oneself and one's] opponent with a kick—to close in safely.

Following the above suggestion will give you endless hours of instruction. Of course, you must use the set system, that is REPETITION of each technique in sets for perfection. You begin now immediately to work on what I mentioned and apply all you've learned with ECONOMY OF MOTION—you will double your speed and skill doing just that.

I hope I have impressed in your mind a most important rule of our style—stick to the program I've given you, use variety, and do not worry too much that your students need more and more to stay with you—true [only] if they can do perfectly all you've taught them.

Remember the idea that one has to come in thousands of times in order to perfect one judo throw. And, of course, use your own experience and imagination. You will do well. I have faith in you.

Bruce

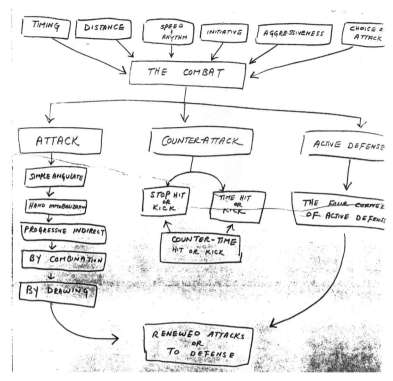

This chart, drafted by Bruce Lee and sent to Taky Kimura about 1967, explains the schematic of combat and features the "five ways of attack" of jeet kune do.

To Taky Kimura

September 11, 1967

Taky,

Quarterly card for Winter (Sept. 21–Dec. 21, 1967). Fill in the rest with typewriter and sign your name on (instructor).

Bruce

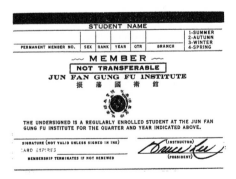

Letters of the Dragon

To Taky Kimura

October 1967

Taky,
Let me know if you've found out about the uniform.

If not, let me know if that Mrs. Mar still makes the vest & badges (somewhere else didn't you say?). At any rate, find out the total cost.

Thank you.

How's everything?

Bruce

To George Lee

October 1967

Dear George,
I'm planning on coming up for Wally's luau and at the same time to go to James' class in Fremont. I understand that the class consists of mostly Chinese.

I'll fly up on Friday (Nov. 3) and James' class is that same night. So if you have nothing previously planned, it might be beneficial for you to attend that class. I'm going to teach a public class—it has been a long time. Say, maybe you can go to the luau, too.

Anyway, I'll talk to you when I'm up there. If you'd like to attend the Fremont class for that night, contact James.

Take care my friend.

Best regards to your wife,

Bruce Lee

To George Lee

Bruce Lee and friends at Wally Jae's luau, November 1967.

November 1967

Dear George,
I'm glad you made it to the Luau. Allen Joe went too, but he couldn't get in.[9] Anyway, I'm glad it's over as I'm sick of demonstrations.

The two punching pads are out of sight and Dan flipped when he saw them. He said it's too beautiful to be used in class. We might as well know that whatever you make, you turn it into a masterpiece. Terrific!

There will be a birthday get-together at my house on Nov. 25, Sat. So let me know if you can make it for that weekend and come up on Friday night (Nov. 24). I'll send you a round trip ticket, so do let me know as soon as you can. Do not tell James or anyone I'm sending you the ticket though.

Again, thank you for your "cool" equipment.

Bruce

P.S. The shoes [with metal soles and toe pieces] are really nicely put together.

To Taky Kimura

November 1967

Taky,
Well, it's Nov. 7 already, and [in] three more weeks we will be getting

together. So as soon as you find out, do let me know of your plans.

Draw money from the club for your plane fare and we can deduct that at the end of the year anyway. So do let me know when you will come down and how long you plan to stay, etc., etc. Let me know.

Any news on the pants yet?

That's all for now.

Take care,

Bruce Lee

To George Lee

Dear George,

Your work, every one of them, is fantastic. Not only are they professional, they are simply artistic. As usual, everyone here has high praise for your art.

I, myself, do appreciate very much for your taking time off to do all those wonderful things for me. Thanks a lot George.

I'm sorry to say that I've lost your list for autographs, so will you please send me another one? Tell Dave Young of the delay, too.

Upon my arrival, my agent called to let me know of CBS' proposal for a one hour serial—kind of like "I Spy" called "Hawaii 5-0." Looks good. I'll let you know what develops.

Bruce

Bruce Lee with Allen Joe (left) and James Yimm Lee (right); the three men had been friends since the early 1960s.

To Taky Kimura

November 1967

Taky,

By now Ed Parker MUST have contacted you. So as soon as you make plane arrangements let me know. James Lee will be coming down too, and also Jhoon Rhee of Washington, DC, will be staying as a guest at the house. So, this coming weekend [there] will be a lot of people at the house.

I'm looking forward to your visit. Also be sure to bring the sample uniform down. It should be ready by now; I wrote you a letter quite a while back asking for it.

So let me know as soon as you can regarding your flight information, plus the uniform.

See you,

Bruce

1968

To George Lee

January 1968

George,
Haven't written for a little while, how are things?

Your wall punching bags have definitely helped in my daily training. I've started the training on Christmas eve—my 1968 resolution. I now train an average of two-and-a-half hours a day, including hand exercises, leg exer-cises, running, isometrics,

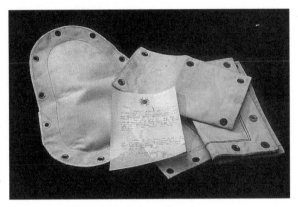

Wall-mounted punching bags George Lee designed and made after Bruce Lee's drawings and descriptions.

stomach exercises, sparring exercises, free-hand exercises. Your training equipment all helps in my program. Thanks.

Allen Joe must have told you about James Lee's surprise party on January 26 (Frid. night)—I'll fly in that night without letting him know. Do your best to be there; after all, you are one of the very important members.

So, take care my friend, and my best to your wife and family.

Bruce

By the way, could you give me your home phone number once more?

To George Lee

February 1968

George,

Enclosed please find the pins of our school. It was nice seeing you

Punching bags with punched holes in each side made by George Lee after Bruce Lee's suggestions.

during my visit and you looked well, as usual.

One idea for the long bag (for kicking) is to make it like the regular punch bag that you made with punched holes in both sides. That way I can lower or make it higher.

When Linda came to pick me up the car had an accident—lucky nobody got hurt. Brandon bumped his head slightly. The car is out for a few days.

> Take care,
> Bruce

To George Lee

February 1968

George,

Will be coming up to Oakland this coming Friday (Feb. 16).

> See you then,
> Bruce

To George Lee

April 1968

George,

Remember the kicking and punching padded boards you made for me—well, after using them for a while I've come to many improve-ments. When you have time, can you make an extra kick-ing board and punching board for me? Your kicking board is tops for kicking, no heavy bag can replace it. The accompa-nying sheets will describe the added improvements.

Steve McQueen, after he completes his movie in Frisco, will get a writer and start on a gung fu movie with him and I in it.[10] So this is a start toward the movie.

On April 6 I probably will come up because there is

Bruce Lee presents a trophy to a young martial artist at Jhoon Rhee's tournament in Washington, D.C. (Jhoon Rhee stands at the center of the group, holding the microphone.)

a so called "National Gung Fu Exhibition," held in Frisco—a bunch of jerks will be in there, including the "runner." I will show up to scare [the] hell out of them.

Take care,

Bruce

P.S. How do you like the new cards—am teaching a few guys private lessons now.

To George Lee

September 26, 1968

George,
I still feel bad about that mixed up date. I thought it was Sept. 29 (Sunday).

I'll be leaving for Mississippi with Steve [McQueen]. The project on jeet kune do as a movie is taking another step. Stirling Silliphant (*In the Heat of the Night*) is involved to write the script. We will be getting together and roll. After that I will be flying to New York for a few days.

Of course in the midst of all this I'm moving, too. As of next Monday my address will be:

2551 Roscomare Rd.
Los Angeles, California 90024

It's a pretty "cool" house, located inside Bel-Air. As soon as I have the phone in, I'll let you know.

Anyway, let me know if you can come down on Nov. 27. Maybe we should arrange it at a different date. At any rate, the next day will be Thanksgiving.

Take care my friend,
Bruce

To George Lee

George, the master maker,
Thanks for those four "magnificent" throwing bags!
Man, they are cool—really cool.
With appreciation,
Bruce

To George Lee

November 1968

George,
I tried like hell, but I just can't get away during the Thanksgiving weekend. I would very much like to come because you're one of my very close friends, I want you to know that.

As soon as I have things clear here—(I have been very busy working)—I would [like to] come up and give you a call.

By the way, James Coburn (*Our Man Flint*) would like to have one of your wall bags. Can you get him one?

Will talk to you soon.

Thank you again for your kind invitation,

Bruce

1969

To William Cheung

Posted from Los Angeles on January 4, 1969

William,

I was looking over my old mail and found most of the letters you wrote me. The latest one, or the latest one that I found, has this address so I write this letter in hopes that even if you moved, somehow or another, this will reach you.

> I've lost faith in the Chinese classical arts...because basically all styles are products of land swimming....My line of training is more toward efficient street fighting with everything goes, wearing head gear, gloves, chest guard, shin/knee guards, etc.

It has been nearly ten years now since I've been in the States and when I sit down some evening lost in my recollection of my memories, you are among one of those that often pop up. I sincerely hope you and your family are enjoying the best of everything.

During the last ten years, Chinese martial art has always been a major part of my activity, though I am now in a new field, the field of acting. My achievement in the martial art is most satisfying and the word "Chinese" has come a long way in the circle of martial art due to the fact that all three of the U.S. karate free-style champs are studying under me.[11]

William, I've lost faith in the Chinese classical arts—though I still call mine Chinese—because basically all styles are products of land swimming, even the Wing Chun school. So my line of training is more toward efficient street fighting with everything goes, wearing head gear, gloves, chest guard, shin/knee guards, etc. For the past five years now I've been training the hardest and for a purpose, not just dissipated hit-miss training. I'm running every day, sometimes up to six miles.

I've named my style jeet kune do—reason for my not sticking to Wing Chun [is] because I sincerely feel that this style has more to offer regarding efficiency. I mentioned all of the above because it is a major event in my life and [I'd] like to fill you in with it.

I've been doing good too in the field of acting. I don't know whether or not you've seen my TV series the "Green Hornet" in Australia, but I've worked for a year in it, setting up a good foundation. Occasionally I appear on TV and movies. The latest

By 1967, Bruce Lee had created a name for his own method of expressing himself through combat and jeet kune do.

one is an MGM production *Little Sister* with James Garner that should be coming out in a few months.[12] I'm in the process of forming a production company with a few important backers here in the States, concentrating on producing martial art movies, TV series, etc.

I've just bought a half acre home in Bel-Air—like living out in the country, but tough on the calves running around the hill side.

Well, my friend, all in all, that's what happened to me—I don't know whether this will reach you. I hope it will.

Anyway, my warmest regards to your family and do drop me a line. I would like to hear from you.

Your friend,

Bruce Lee

To William Cheung

January 20, 1969

Glad to know you're living at the same address.

You remembered correctly, I have a 4-year old son and one expected this coming April. I am truly a lucky man to have a wonderful wife and a most harmonious family.

Do let me know if you and your wife are planning for a visit here in the States. You two are most welcome to stay at my house. Of course, my students and associates would just love to see your talent in Wing Chun and your "abstract field of self-defense." They are a wonderful group of matured, groovy people from all branches of un-rhythmic art, street fighters, boxers-kickers, etc., etc.

Really, martial art is not for the masses. This is what I feel and I do think that you should keep to yourself your very own "abstract field operational research, etc.," and don't let anyone know. After all, as you pointed out in your letter you have spent a full three long years on it. Keep it to yourself and close friends. I am sure you will one day come up with something even more soul-gratifying [in] structure. My best wishes go to that.

So you're getting a degree in Economics & Statistics! Well, congratulations! I wish you all the success in it and that it will bring you much enjoyment.

Take good care my friend, and have fun.
Bruce

To George Lee

George,
After experimenting on the shield, we find that because of the thickness and extra weight, it absorbs the shock much better. Therefore, the holder is not as miserable as before, thanks to you.

As I mentioned, we are preparing a script, Coburn, Silliphant and I. Coburn and I will star in it. We hope to start shooting [at] the end of the year, if Coburn's schedule is open. If not, then it has to be next March. At any rate, this will be the start of something really, really big for me.

Take care my friend and thank you once more,

Bruce

To Jhoon Goo Rhee[13]

Tuesday, March 4, 1969

To Mr. Jhoon Goo,

The purpose of this letter is twofold: First, to show off the typewriter; second, to keep you up on the latest here in the West.

We had a meeting on Project "Leng" last Friday, Coburn, Stirling, and I. Project "Leng" is a code name for our martial art motion picture. *Leng* is a Chinese word meaning beautiful. Anyway, there is a big breakthrough. Stirling didn't mind his nephew Mark being taken off the writing job, and him and Coburn are both in [agreement] to hire a professional to do the job. We will speed up the process as soon as the writer comes up with the treatment.

We will have another meeting this coming week. Everything is going big gun. Also, Stirling is preparing another film, and he wants me to be his associate producer and technical advisor for the picture—a Japanese samurai picture. Coburn might be in it, too. It will be three months work in Japan. If things go smoothly, the picture can start in six months, then after that, our picture, project "Leng," beautiful, beautiful indeed.

I might go on that publicity tour for MGM yet, though they are not too happy with the money I asked.[14] We will see. If I should go, I will get you on with me for publicity for your school, especially on National TV.

Remember my friend, everything goes to those who aim to get. Low aim is the biggest crime a man has. One will never get any more than he thinks he can get. You have what it takes. Look back and see your progress—damn the torpedo, full speed ahead!

By the way, *Black Belt* called and asked me for additional information on your school. You can rest assured that what I filled in had to make your school the greatest *dojo* there is. The fact that you are the most generous furnisher of decorations, 'around' three thousand dollars rent, etc., etc., I can't even remember what I told the secretary.

Delgado opened a school here. He will compete in Parker's tournament next week, so is Joe Lewis.[15] Lewis' latest wish is to become a professional boxer.

Well my friend, take good care and my best regards to Han Soong and the family.

By the way, how is little "abagee?"

Bruce

To Jhoon Goo Rhee

Jhoon Goo,

Thank you for your wonderful gift to my son, he sleeps with the bear nowadays.[16]

Enclosed I'm rushing the ad & information where you can obtain the gain weight food supplements. Be sure to order it from York, PA, instead of from Los Angeles, California, as there is a difference in postage.

Add peanuts, eggs (with shells) and bananas into the powder with milk and mix them in a blender. If you really want faster results use "half and half" instead of ordinary milk.

The postman is here, I better mail this. Talk to you later.

Your friend,

Bruce Lee

To Jhoon Goo Rhee

Jhoon Goo,
Enclosed please find [Chuck] Norris' ad. This is the most recent
one. I'll try to save them for you in the future. Also, I have included
other ads of similar nature, which might be of help.

*[Bruce Lee included this poem, which he wrote to help encourage his old
friend, advising him not to let adverse circumstances affect him and to
realize that each individual controls his own destiny.]*

WHO AM I?
Who am I?
That is the age-old question
Asked by every man
At one time or another.
Though he looks into a mirror
And recognizes the face,
Though he knows his own name
And age and history,
Still he wonders, deep down,
Who am I?
Am I a giant among men,
Master of all I survey,
Or an ineffectual pygmy
Who clumsily blocks his own way?
Am I the self-assured gentleman
With a winning style,
The natural born leader
Who makes friends instantly,
Or the frightened heart
Tiptoeing among strangers,
Who, behind a frozen smile, trembles
Like a little boy lost in a dark forest?

Most of us yearn to be one,
But fear we are the other.
Yet we CAN be
What we aspire to be.
Those who cultivate
Their natural instincts,
Who set their sights
On the good, the admirable, the excellent,
And believe they can achieve it
Will find their confidence rewarded.
And, in the process,
They will discover the true identity
Of him who looks back from the mirror.
WHICH ARE YOU?
The doubters said,
"Man cannot fly,"
The doers said,
"Maybe, but we'll try,"
And finally soared
Into the morning's glow,
While non-believers
Watched from below.
The doubters claimed
The world was flat,
Ships plunged over its edge,
And that was that!
Yet a brand new world
Some doers found,
And returned to prove
This planet round.
The doubters knew
'Twas fact, "Of course,
No noisy gadget

Letters of the Dragon

Would e'er replace the horse."
Yet the carriages
Of doers, sans equine,
Came to traverse
All our roads in time
But those who kept saying
"It can't be done,"
Never are the victories
Or the honors won.
But, rather,
By the believing, doing kind,
While the doubters
Watched from far behind.

In conclusion, may I warn you that negativeness very often unknowingly creeps up upon us. It helps occasionally to stop all thoughts (the chattering of worries, anticipations, etc. in your head) and then once more refreshingly march bravely on.

Just as the maintaining of good health may require the taking of unpleasant medicine, so the condition of being able to do the things we enjoy often requires the performance of a few we don't. Remember my friend that it is not what happens that counts, it is how you react to them.

You have what it takes, I know you will win out one way or the other. So damn the torpedo, full speed ahead! Remember what this Chinaman says, "Circumstances? Hell, I make circumstances!"

Peace and harmony,

Bruce

To George Lee

June 11, 1969

George,

A letter to let you know that Coburn's picture should be on its way next week.[17] I just returned from the East coast with him. McQueen is in Europe, so his has to wait. Just want to let you know I haven't forgotten my friend.

My mother and brother are here. They are presently staying with me.

Things are going great with me—will let you know when they develop.

Take care,

Bruce

To Jhoon Goo Rhee

June 25, 1969

Jhoon,

Had lunch with Mito this afternoon.[18] At a glance, I can see you are mentioned in both upcoming B.B.[19] and the new *Karate Illustrated* [magazines] (a picture of you awarding a belt to Skipper in the Mullins story).[20] The Nationals has good "pictorial coverage" and I think "Letters to the Editor" mentions your branch in Dominican Republic—so, all in all, good coverage, especially the Nationals.

Also, I talked to Mito about your book. I told him it will be "quality" and he definitely likes to look over it. Well, I have bridged the gap, the rest is up to you. You can call him directly if you like.

Remember the article you sent on kicking? Well, that was not enough, but they want to do it now with eight people or somewhere around that, like Oshima, Ark Yu Wong, Sea Oh Choi, some Okinawa instructors, etc., etc. The topic will be on the various kicks, the side, the round house, the heel, etc., etc.

Anyway, if your discussion with Mito on your book proves to be successful, you might be able to come out to do the article and "represent" tae kwon do, or the Korean version of the kicking. It will be a prestiged moment with the various representatives and also to establish you as the spokesman for the Korean style.

Your mental attitude determines what you make of it, as stepping or stumbling block. Remember, no man is really defeated unless he is discouraged.

Personally I have all the confidence in your backing up the kicking quality with any of them present.

Anyway, give me a call and let me know how your discussion with Mito comes out.

Bruce

To Jhoon Goo Rhee

Jhoon Goo,

Just had lunch with Mito this afternoon. I have further sold him on the value of your chest protector. Subtly, I have fed him with ideas on the protector and I'm pretty sure he has a favorable attitude even before he has seen the merchandise.

Mito, as you probably know, now handles only the magazine. His brother Jim handles the mail order business. However, I have made suggestions for him to talk personally to you first. When things are agreed upon you can then transact arrangements with Jim. Mito would be the person to start, and he does have a most favorable attitude toward you. More than once he has remarked that he likes you.

Anyway, I just want to let you know how things are, and also I like you to know that the 1969 Nationals was a stepping stone and not a stumbling block. Your mental attitude determines what you make of it, as stepping or stumbling block. Remember, no man is really defeated unless he is discouraged.

As a side observer, I know you have done your part right, and though the outcome of the tournament was not quite up to standard, you did everything right. It is not what happens that is success or failure, but what it does to the heart of man.

You have that quality of being active, awake, pushing ahead at all times, and always ahead of the other tournament directors in terms of services, knowledge and truthfulness. The last quality, I feel, definitely demands cooperation from your fellow colleagues.

I wrote this not because I am cheering you up, maybe I am, but I want you to know that when the mean is in order, the end is ultimately inevitable. What you must not do now is to worry and think of the Nationals that is now of the past.

What you HABITUALLY THINK largely determines what you will ultimately become. Remember, success is a journey, not a destination. I have faith in your ability. You will do just fine.

Take care,
Bruce

To Siu Hon-san[21]

July 1969

Uncle Siu:
I have mentioned you and your Chinese pugilistic teaching in Hong Kong to *Black Belt* magazine. It is the greatest gung fu magazine in America. It reports on martial arts of the whole world, including karate, hapkido, judo and so on. Internationally known teachers always appear in it.

If you are interested, you can write a short history of martial arts and your philosophy of boxing and send it to me together with photographs. I can translate them into English. With publicity in *Black Belt* magazine, it may be of some help when you come to America.

I've recommended you to *Black Belt* magazine, so they want to write a biography about you. If you are interested, you can send your photographs and your articles to "*Black Belt* Magazine" in care of me, as follows:

Black Belt, Inc.
c/o Bruce Lee
5650 W. Washington Blvd.
Los Angeles, Calif. 90016
My temporary address is:
P.O. Box 5109
Beverly Hills
Calif. 90210
It's because I have bought a new house.

To Leo Fong

Leo,
Here are some historical facts on the CHOY LAY FUT style. Remember that the terms are mainly of Cantonese origin. They are difficult to obtain; took me some time.

Choy lay fut was founded by Chan Heung in Kwang Tung Province. Like many of the Southern Chinese youths, he was first introduced to the popular southern sil lum style of hung kuen by his uncle. Later on, he trained with a Lay (or Lee) Yau Saan. Still yearning for more knowledge, he went to Mt. Law Fow and sought out the Monk Choy Fook.

Before long, Chan Heung was to combine all his learning to form his own style, and named it the choy lay fut style. To honor his previous instructors, he named his style after them. *Choy* was named after Monk Choy Fook, *Lay*, after Lay Yau Saan, and finally, because Hung Kuen is one of the many branches of the Sil Lum Buddhist Temple, thus the term *fut* (Buddhist) is adopted.

Choy lay fut is essentially a long-range style of boxing, relying on a strong "horse" (stance), and is known for its joint-locking techniques, the backfist, the downward swing and the knuckle fist.

There are many empty-hand sets (forms) in this Southern style: the long-range fist, Buddhist fist, t'ai, ping, teen gok fists, etc. In weapon sets there are baat gwa lance (pa-kua), willow leaf, double swords, eighteen staff, etc.

Among the more famous practitioners of this style were Chang Hung Sing, the leading disciple of the founder Chan Heung. Presently, many of the choy lay fut training halls are also known as *hung sing kwoon* (kwoon = training hall). Chang's own leading disciple by the name of Chan Sing was quite a popular Chinese-boxing instructor in Fut Saan of Southern China. Tam Saam was another able choy lay fut practitioner.

Well enough of theoretical information, got to tune up my body.

Warm regards,

Bruce

1970

To Wong Shun-Leung[22]

January 11, 1970

Dear Shun-leung,

It has been a long time since I last wrote to you. How are you? Alan Shaw's letter from Canada asks me to lend you my 8mm film. I am sorry about that. It is because I have lost it when I moved my home. That film is already very old and I seldom use it, so I have lost it. I am sorry for it.

Now I have bought a house in Bel-Air. It is about half an acre. There are many trees. It has the taste of a range. It is located on a hill top near Beverly Hills. Moreover, besides my son Brandon, I have had a daughter, Shannon, who is seven months old. Have you re-married? Please send my regards to your sisters.

Recently, I have organized a film production company. I have also written a story "The Silent Flute." James Coburn and I will act in it. Stirling Silliphant is the screen play writer. He is a famous screen play writer (*In the Heat of the Night*). We plan to make the first martial arts film in Hollywood. The prospect is good. About six months from now, the filming work will begin. All who participate in this film are my students. In the future, Steve McQueen may also work together with me. I am very excited about this plan.

As to martial art, I still practice daily. I teach my students and friends twice a week. It doesn't matter if they are Western boxers, tae kwon do practitioners or wrestlers, I will teach them as long as they are friendly and will not get uptight.

Since I started to practice realistically in 1966 (protectors, gloves, etc.) I feel that I had many prejudices before, and they are wrong. So I changed the name of the gist of my study to jeet kune do. Jeet kune do is only a name. The most important thing is to avoid having bias in training. Of course, I run every day, I practice my tools (punch, kick, throw, etc.). I have to raise the basic conditions daily. Although the principle of boxing is important, practicality is even more important.

I thank you and Master [Yip Man] for teaching me the ways of Wing Chun in Hong Kong. Actually, I have to thank you for leading me to walk on a practical road. Especially in the States, there are Western boxers, I often practice with them, too. There are many so-called masters in Wing Chun here, I really hope that they will not be so blind [as] to fight with those Western boxers!

I may make a trip to Hong Kong. I hope that you are still living in the same place. We are intimate friends, we need to meet more and chat about our past days. That will be a lot of fun, don't you think? When you see Master Yip, please send my regards to him.

Happiness be with you,
Bruce Lee

To Jhoon Goo Rhee

The following letter was written by Bruce Lee to his friend Jhoon Rhee with some ideas on how to produce a television show on self-defense for women.

Jhoon Goo,
Here are some thoughts that enter my mind after our phone conversation.

Background for Program
  A) Light Oriental background music which becomes louder before and after program.

B) The setting has to be simple Oriental design with mats and all—most important your own school emblem (big!) in the background.

Costumes

A) You the head instructor wear gi at all time.[23]

B) The lady wears different street clothes.

Situation

A) Realistic duplication of actual attack (Note: whoever the attacker, he must be fierce and rough toward his victim).

B) Provide props as much as possible to capture the street scene—like chair, phony car, etc., etc.

Lessons

1. Take one technique at a time and show it from different angles and perspectives so as not to make the lesson monotonous.

2. Needless to say, the program has to be both educational and entertaining—realize the fact that [being] too educational will make the show too dull; on the other hand, too entertaining will decrease the martial art spirit. However, though a happy medium is desired, for a TV program, do lean toward showmanship.

3. Besides your usual lesson plans, do give brief lectures on safety at home, in a car, walking alone on the street, etc., etc.

4. Do take advantage of current [news]paper clippings of attacks so as to instill fear that will lead to taking actual lessons. Get as much statistics as you can on crimes, attacks, etc. and report it on the air.

5. Definitely encourage the viewer to write in.

6. As the program goes on, you should sell some of your products—books, or whatever items you feel would help the ladies.

Some Things to be Considered

1. You must secure ownership of your film pilot no matter [if] it sells or not.

2. Make your program a package deal with you as the hiring force for whatever assistants you have on the show.

3. I would recommend—if it does not conflict with policy—that you have the girl plus the attackers so that you become the principle of the show while those two are demonstrators. Of course you will occasionally demonstrate on the attacker as to the proper and correct way of execution.

4. Have [the] lawyer consult the Screen Guild as to [the] Union's policy on your type of show. Do this when concrete deal is being made.

What more can I say at this time but to wish you the best and hope the show will materialize. Should I come up with any more ideas, I'll write you.

See if you can make pilot here in the West coast. I should be of help.

Bruce

A hand-held kicking and punching board made by George Lee after the design and suggestions of Bruce Lee

To George Lee

George,

A masterpiece indeed!

My appreciation my friend—not only to the workmanship (that is always tops!) but particularly to your thoughtfulness.

Thank you, George.

Peace-Love-Brotherhood,

Bruce

To William Cheung

February 18, 1970

Dear William,

It is indeed a surprise to hear from you. Sorry to hear about your job in [the] Bureau of Census & Statistics; hope you have better luck in your next job. I'm sure you will land the most appropriate and gratifying job before long.

Regarding your friend "Sunny Ho"—I'm afraid without proper papers (which are necessary for employment) he would not go long. Plus the fact that Boston is thousands of miles away from here. I am in no power to help.

I guess you didn't know that two years ago I closed my three schools and concentrated on my film involvement and self-improvement. You learn a lot during teaching; however, seeing is not enough, you must do; knowing is not enough, you must apply. So here I'm back to enjoying my training and do some private lessons occasionally.

By the way, I'm doing a film *The Silent Flute* for Warner Bro. this fall in India. The picture is based on martial art and will be released in '72. You should enjoy it. I wrote the original story. The screenplay is a joint effort, headed by Stirling Silliphant (*In the Heat of the Night*), a most able screen writer here in Hollywood.

In closing, let me once more offer my best wishes and may the journey ahead be a most harmonious one for you.

Warm regards,

Bruce

To Linda[24]

Posted from Gstaad, Switzerland, on February 20, 1970

Linda,

This letter would have gone to you much, much sooner. You see, I took some U.S. air-letters with me and wrote you while I was in Geneva. Of course, to my dismay, they just do not accept U.S. letters to be mailed from Switzerland. So, here I am writing once more.

First of all, the journey was very tiring. Switzerland is indeed quite different from the States, and Gstaad is THE RESORT for THE very rich. I have [not] yet met one person that does not have a couple of houses, or chalets as they call them. Of course I went skiing today with Roman and though I had a few falls, everybody thought I adapted to it great. Anyway, all in all, it has been not quite as enjoyable though [it has been quite] an experience being in Europe.

They, the few friends of Roman who stay at the same house, are the so-called jet set, and they are stoned practically all the time, and they are kind of silly. Roman, if not skiing, is always after some girls. Luckily there is one martial art nut here in town, and he will show me around whenever Roman is off. All in all, the group is not my type, and for once I'm looking at the jet set from inside out.

I'm definitely planning to stop by London on my way back to see Ngan Jai.[25] By the way, before I forget, I'm supposed to teach Sy this coming Tues. DO remember to call and let him know I'll make it the following Tuesday. . . .

It's 12:30 AM and the change of hour is still disturbing my balance. At any rate, I like you to know you are often in my thoughts and that you are indeed a wonderful and lovely wife. Say hello to the kids for me and hope this letter reaches you before Sy's appointment. At any rate, do call him and leave a message or explain to him.

Love,

Bruce

                                                    Letters of the Dragon

P.S. I was going to write my mother again (I wrote in U.S. air letter) and I tore this open, thinking it was the U.S. letter.

To Linda

Posted from Gstaad, Switzerland, on February 23, 1970

Linda,

To start off, I want to say I really miss my wife and that I love her. From what I have seen [of the] people coming in and out of Roman's chalet, my appreciation of you grows. The so-called jet set is really boring to [the] extent that they all go to extremes. Just keeping company with the whole group going to night clubs tired me out. Loss of sleep is a common event for me since I'm here, either stuck at some people's house waiting for Roman to pick me up, or wanting to leave but couldn't.

To put it short, I'm kind of fed up and want very, very much to be with my family. When I come back, I'll tell you of Gstaad and its rich people.

Well, I hope you have received my postcard and letter. I have another postcard of Gstaad, but I have left it in my coat pocket, and it's bent and screwed up.

First chance I feel justified, I'll leave and hope to stop by London and take a quick visit to Ngan Jai. At any rate, things are just a big sitting on your ass and listening to blasting noisy music here. To top it, I have a cold sore and well. . . .

However, I'm adapting to the flow and you don't have to worry about my boredom. There are a few nice "human" [beings] here that I can relate to. Karate enthusiasts.

Love,

Bruce

To Linda

Posted from Gstaad, Switzerland, on February 26, 1970

Linda,

The cold weather and sleepless nights have finally taken their toll. I caught the flu and it's miserably weakening, especially teaching two lessons a day. Luckily it is nothing like the H.K. flu that I had. The doctor came last night and prescribed some medications. I'm improving and am in bed all day and night, except [when] teaching.

It looks like I'll be back on Tuesday. At any rate, I'll call when I arrive in New York. I'm looking forward to coming home. It's hot inside the house and cold outside and I'm tired of the environment. Roman treated me real nice, but his way of living just isn't mine. Late eating and late sleeping.

Anyway, I'm tired and need rest.

See you soon.

Love always,

Bruce

To Linda

Posted from Gstaad, Switzerland, on February 27, 1970

Linda,

Everybody is out skiing and I am alone with the cook, Rick. He's really a good cook. Anyway, I want to write to let you know I have recovered and you need not worry. I was down but I feel myself now.

I'm leaving for London tomorrow and hope to stay there for a couple of days, to buy a pair of boots, and to see Ngan Jai. Hopefully I can see the town. I'll be staying at Roman's house, and his friend, a director also, might pick me up. If not, I'll have to take a bus into town and then a taxi to Roman's house.

I can tell you one thing, I'm dying to come home. Yet I feel I must stop by London as I have never been there and this is such an opportunity I mustn't miss. Anyway, I want you to know that I miss you.

I wrote to Jim to explain to him that since Roman sent for me from such a long way, I'm obliged to stay. I hope him and Stirling are working out in earnest on our story.

When I come back I'll have a lot of interesting tales to tell. At any rate, this trip has been interesting, observing various people coming in and out of the house.

One thing for sure, I got to know Roman a little bit more, and I feel this will help future developments. If not, at least [I] have a friend, and a student. He has improved in his performance.

I [would] like to be back on Tuesday, March 3rd, and, believe me, Roman wants me to stay on and on.

Well my dearest, take good care of yourself and say hello to my son Brandon and do kiss Shannon for me.

Love you!!!

Bruce

To Linda[26]

Posted from Kowloon, Hong Kong, on March 29, 1970, at 7:00 PM

Linda,

First of all Brandon wants me to relate to you his message to you. Here goes:

> "Roses are red. Violets are blue.
> Sugar is sweet and so are you."
> We arrived 3 min. earlier. . . got to listen to cartoon on ear
>   phone. . . .

Here goes: Brandon is getting along just fine, enjoying all the special privileges. He did not wet at all now for 4 nights. And, of course, no diapers. Well, we'll see soon. . . .

I'm recognized everywhere as Lee Shiu Loong, "Kato," especially with my clothing and Brandon.

Also, everyone is asking for favors nowadays, getting them into U.S. show business or getting over to the States, or appearing on shows.

Brandon is eating only Western food and definitely HATES the milk here. I have given special instructions as to regular meals but of course goodies somehow always find their way into his stomach. He is showing off in front of everybody and enjoys every minute of it. However, we both DO miss you a lot.

With love always,

Bruce

To Linda

Posted from Kowloon, Hong Kong,
on April 2, 1970, at 10:00 AM

April 1, 1970

Linda,
Received your letter dated "Saturday
night." First of all, Brandon has been very
nice indeed. Even the problem of not eating—when he first arrived—is gradually
solved. Let me tell you "our routine."

We usually get up at around six, and
together we take a bath. Of course he will
climb to my bed—we stay in the same
room—and "me-me" me.[27] By the way,
I've just given him a big "me-me" for you.

Bruce and Brandon Lee prepare for
their departure for Hong Kong in 1970.

Then he goes to get dressed while I dry
my hair. Then we go out and have breakfast (this is a daily routine).
He follows my mother willingly and you should know why. He has
all kinds of toys now. . . .

My mother is extremely nice to me, too, as she has bought a
great amount of fantastic gifts for me. Hope I can get through [U.S.
customs] without [a] tax problem. Wait till you see them. By the
way, among them [is] a "really" beautiful 12-person China dishes
from Kwang Hsi, famous for its China. Phoebe has to bring them
for me. All I can say is, wait till you see what I have bought.
Haven't spent one cent of my money yet.

Obtained your measurements in your letter. Phoebe might
have to bring them, as [when going through customs,] women's
clothing in my personal belongings might mess up my already filled
Chinese clothings.

I usually go to tea with Mr. Tse daily. Mrs. Tso's mother-in-law is dying and she is at the hospital daily.

I might appear on TV providing there is enough time for me. There are many requests.

I think—no, I know—this trip has done Brandon good and he is very happy. Of course he has "me-me" me a lot since you are not here. I, too, am very glad and fortunate to be able to share my life with you. You are fantastic and I love you dearly though my nature does not show it as frequently as I should.

I love you,
Bruce

To Linda

Posted from Kowloon, Hong Kong, on April 4, 1970, at 10:00 AM

April 3, 1970

Linda,
Brandon wants to write you a poem again:
    "Hurray! Hurray!
    Today is May!"

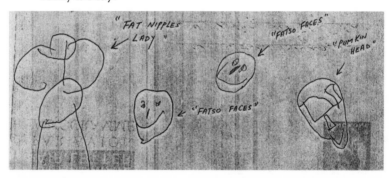

Sketches by Brandon, with his captions inserted by Bruce; this sheet was included with Bruce's April 3, 1970, letter to Linda.

We have just returned from the amusement park and Brandon Lee had a wonderful, wonderful time. He is enjoying himself tremendously and aside from forcing him to eat something, he has been a very good boy and everyone here loves him. I have devoted time for him daily, and he follows my mother "willingly."

I'll be appearing on two or three TV shows here in H.K. starting next week. Everyone here looks up to me. I also enjoy my stay here as I have the opportunity to talk to my friends (Mr. Tse, Mr. Ng, etc.) during the daily tea time.[28]

That Greek wrote me and definitely requests me to teach him [for] a week in Paris. I can tell you one thing, it won't be in the near future, I'm tired of traveling.

Tonight I'll begin my shaping up program at Mr. Shaw's gym as I have to appear on TV this coming Tuesday. I have been getting up early nowadays. This is mainly due to [the] time change and "me-me" boy.

I'm looking forward very much to return home. Though Brandon does not show it (toys, playing around, etc., etc.) I'm sure he is looking forward to being with you. He has taken me to be the "me-me" target.

Father and son are both enjoying our togetherness and definitely looking forward to your joining us soon.

Keep well, my love to you and my little girl Shannon.

Love,

Bruce

To Linda[29]

Linda,

Would have waited but my back is bothering me again for these last few days. Hope you don't have to work after next month.

May all go well.

Love,

Bruce

To Hamilton Lee, in Kowloon, Hong Kong

Dear Hamilton,

It has been a long time since we last corresponded. My mother and Robert both have arrived in America and they have mentioned that they have seen you quite a bit.

The last time I returned to Hong Kong you were not there, so I had no chance of seeing you. How are you?

I'm filming in America at present and it's going well. The reason I was very well received the last time that I was in Hong Kong is because I have a deep understanding of action films as a result of 1. what I've learned from the American film industry and 2. my understanding of martial art.

Therefore, I have thought about returning to Hong Kong to make a movie. I'm very enthused but, unfortunately, I've been used. I know if I go to [Hong Kong to] make movies, I will be successful. Unfortunately, up to this point, all of the invitations to do so have been:

1) Manufactured gossip
2) Empty Promises
3) Deceptions, etc.

Why is it that the people in Hong Kong do not have one single individual that, in an honest and decent fashion, can have the capability to use his farsight to create?

Is it true that there is not one business man who can be involved in a fair deal?

To George Lee

December 22, 1970

George,
A personal letter to thank you for your immediate sending of the padding.

Also, I've given that punching pad to Delgado and he expressed his appreciation. As soon as I get around to give him your address, he would like to write to thank you.

So my friend, have a merry Christmas and definitely a rewarding new year.

Again, thank you kindly.

Warm regards,

Bruce

Notes

1. "Dan" is probably Dan Inosanto, who was not only Bruce Lee's good friend, but also assistant instructor at his Los Angeles Chinatown school.

2. Greenway Productions was the company that produced "The Green Hornet."

3. These photos can be found on pages 70, 71, and 96 of *The Tao of Gung Fu* (vol. 2 in the Bruce Lee Library; Boston: Charles E. Tuttle Co., 1997).

4. The following letters were written when Linda visited Seattle, leaving Bruce to look after things at home.

5. Ted Wong was foremost among Bruce Lee's private students. Please see his foreword to *Jeet Kune Do: Bruce Lee's Commentaries on the Martial Way* (vol. 3 in the Bruce Lee Library Series; Boston: Charles E. Tuttle Co., 1997) for more on his relationship with Bruce Lee.

6. The finger bowl was a beautifully constructed silver container made by George Lee. It held sand and/or beans into which fingers were thrust in order to strengthen their penetrative and thrusting power. The outside of the bowl featured a very intricately detailed metalwork engraving of a dragon, which symbolizes not only Bruce Lee's Chinese stage name, but also Chinese zodiac symbol for the year of his birth.

7. The "book" was—at this juncture—*The Tao of Gung Fu.* As his martial evolution progressed, he eventually decided not to publish this book and instead began working on *The Tao of Jeet Kune Do,* a book that more accurately reflected his martial beliefs from 1967 onward. Both books have subsequently been published by the Charles E. Tuttle Company as volumes 2 and 3, respectively, in the Bruce Lee Library.

8. Although this letter is not dated, it was probably written between September and October of 1967, several months after Bruce Lee opened his Chinatown school in Los Angeles.

9. Allen Joe was one of Bruce Lee's earliest students and close friends from Oakland, California. Apart from being a talented martial artist, Allen was also an experienced bodybuilder of considerable repute, and helped introduce Bruce to the benefits of weight training.

10. Steve McQueen was in San Francisco filming the movie *Bullitt.*

11. The three United States karate freestyle champs were Chuck Norris, Joe Lewis, and Mike Stone.

12. Later retitled *Marlowe* and released by Metro-Goldwyn-Mayer.

13. Jhoon Rhee is considered the "Father of Tae Kwon Do" in North America and was a close friend of Bruce Lee, who appeared at many of Rhee's martial art tournaments in Washington, DC, and often wrote to encourage Rhee in his many martial art–related projects.

14. MGM was looking to send Bruce Lee on a press junket to promote *Marlowe,* in which he had a cameo appearance.

15. Louis Delgado was a point karate champion who studied for a time under Bruce Lee. Delgado once beat Chuck Norris for the Grand Championship in New York. Ed Parker is considered one of the foremost martial artists in North America and the "father of American Kenpo."

16. Jhoon Rhee had purchased a teddy bear for Brandon.

17. George Lee had requested an autographed photo of Bruce Lee's celebrity student, James Coburn.

18. Mito Uyehara, the publisher of *Black Belt* magazine

19. *Black Belt* magazine.

20. Skipper Mullins, one of the top point karate fighters of the era.

21. Siu Hon-san was an older martial artist who had known Bruce Lee since his youth in Hong Kong. In referring to Siu Hon-san as "uncle," Bruce Lee employs a common Chinese method of showing respect to a friend or associate who is older.

22. Wong Shun-Leung was a senior student of Yip Man. During Lee's early years in the martial arts, in addition to being a close friend, from time to time he was also a tutor.

23. A *gi* is a traditional outfit for Japanese martial art (typically karate and/or judo) consisting of top, pants, and belt.

24. Since developments were slow in Hollywood, Bruce Lee had returned to teaching. Rather than teach publicly, an approach he found to be ineffective for helping students make the most of their abilities, he gave private lessons. His clients included the very rich (who paid up to $275 an hour and $1,000 a week) as well as lower- and middle-income earners (whom he charged nothing at all, but who were,

like him, sincere in their quest to "discover the cause of their own ignorance"). One of Bruce's wealthier clients was certainly film director Roman Polanski, whose wife, Sharon Tate, he had also taught. In 1970, Polanski asked Bruce Lee to instruct him in Gstaad, Switzerland.

25. Ngan Jai (a.k.a. Wu Ngan) was the son of one of the servants to the Lee family while Bruce was growing up. For a number of years, Bruce Lee's father looked after him as if he were one of his own children. As he was approximately the same age as Bruce, the two became friends, and stayed in touch throughout Bruce's life. In fact, when Bruce, Linda, and the children moved to Hong Kong in 1971, Ngan Jai and his wife and children were invited to move in in exchange for helping out around the house.

26. In 1970, Bruce took his five-year-old son Brandon to visit his family in Hong Kong, and also to share in a father-son traveling experience.

27. According to Linda Lee Cadwell, whenever young Brandon wanted attention, he would run up to someone and excitedly say, "me-me, me-me!"

28. Mr. Tse and Mr. Ng were Cantonese film stars from Bruce's childhood.

29. Bruce Lee hurt his lower back quite severely in 1970. With no steady work in Hollywood, and his injury preventing him from practicing, Linda had to work evenings in order to help support the family. This, of course, distressed him even more, as he felt it was his duty to provide for his family. He wrote this note one evening during this period.

嘉禾電影(香港)有限公司
GOLDEN HARVEST (HK) LIMITED

香港九龍彌敦道東英大廈一四一二室
1412, Tung Ying Bldg., 100, Nathan Rd., Kowloon, Hong Kong

Tel. K-672144 (4 Lines)
Cable Add. "GOLDENSUN"

October 28th, 1971

Mr. Ted Ashley
Warner Brothers Studios
Burbank, California
U.S.A.

Dear Ted,

I have talked to my lawyer Mr. Adrian Marshall about Warner's proposal. Since we are friend, I have chosen to write you directly.

In addition to our agreement we feel:-

(a) that I should have a minimum of 4 months off
    a year to make features in Hong Kong

(b) that I should have a participation in
    (1) The T.V. series itself
    (2) merchandizing.

Shooting is running smoothly here and the last picture I made in Thailand has just been released and is on its way to break all records in Hong Kong— damn the torpedo, full speed ahead!!

Take care and best regards to Linda.

Peace

Bruce

Bruce

Part 4

A STAR BEGINS TO RISE

(1971–1972)

1971

To His Wife, Linda

From India in February 1971[1*]

Linda,

I'm writing in a car with Stirling [Silliphant] and Jim [Coburn] going through India—we will be sitting [for] around 16 hours in

Caro, and plus all the sitting on the plane, it's pretty rough on my back. However, I usually get over the "nagging" over night.

Anyway, it's quite an experience for me. I wish you will be able to join me during shooting, and it looks like a pretty definite thing. I hope my mother will not be working then and be able to come stay with the children for India is not a healthy place for kids.

A break during the Indian scouting trip for The Silent Flute—from left: Silliphant, Lee, Coburn, and their guide.

So that means you probably will go through London and hopefully I can arrange to have a driver for you so you may stay a day or two there shopping or what not.

At any rate, we are now heading toward the desert (we've been riding for 4 hrs. now) and the weather is getting hot. Of course, night time will be cold.

The last town we stayed (Jaipur) we were staying in a palace

---

*Notes for Part 4 begin on page 172.

[that has been] converted [into a] hotel and we had the royal quarters. The estate is two miles long—will tell you more when I come back.

Well, I'll stop here as writing in the car begins to affect me. Believe me the road is "terrible!" and the driving is a "nightmare"—wait till you experience it.

The three Americans being feted by their Indian hosts: far left, *Silliphant*; center, *Bruce Lee*; far right, *Coburn*.

To Leo Fong[2]

Leo,

Received your book by Perls, will read it soon.[3]

Silent Flute is moving along fine. We ran into some problems in location, but we should know real soon on the official date.

More exciting still are several developing possibilities which I will tell you when the moment comes.

I'd love to use your "drawing course"—in fact, I was thinking at one time of joining, but if you have it, fine![4]

Due to my back, I have to say I am not in my best of shape; however, my JKD is something else—with adversity you are shocked to higher levels, much like a rain storm that is so violent, but yet afterwards all plant grows. More and more I pity the martial artists that are blinded by their partiality and ignorance.

Will do an article for *Black Belt* as soon as I can find time. The India trip wiped me out. By the way, hope your books will do good, if there is any help I can render for your future books, feel free to ask.

Got to go now. Say hello to your wife for me and take care.

Bruce

To Jhoon Goo Rhee

•

Jhoon Goo,

Greetings from Los Angeles where, like many places in the States, business is not too good. Don't misunderstand me that this is a pessimistic statement, though the fact is just as it is, but like anybody else, you have your choice of reacting to it. Here I ask you Jhoon Goo, are you going to make your obstacles stepping stones to your dreams, or stumbling blocks because unknowingly you let negativeness, worries, fear, etc., to take over you?

Believe me that in every big thing or achievement there is always obstacles, big or small, and the reaction one shows to such obstacles is what counts, not the obstacle itself. There is no such thing as defeat until you admit so yourself, but not until then!

My friend do think of the past in terms of those memories of events and accomplishments which were pleasant, rewarding and satisfying. The present? Well, think of it in terms of challenges and opportunities, and the rewards available for the application of your talents and energies. As for the future, that is a time and a place where every worthy ambition you possess is within your grasp.

You have a tendency to waste a lot of your energy in worry and anticipation. Remember my friend to enjoy your planning as well as your accomplishment, for life is too short for negative energy.

Since the India trip my back is so-so. *Silent Flute* is still on with Warner Bros. We are waiting to hear the next step, and should know within ten days—approval of new budget, setting up another survey trip, etc. Aside from *Silent Flute*, I will do a guest appearance on a new TV series "Longstreet" for next season. Then there is another movie that I will do (one of the three leading characters) should the presentation be approved, and that we should know within ten days or so, too.

Of course the damn thing is I want to do something now! So I have created a TV series idea and I should know within a couple of weeks.[5] In the meantime, I am working on another idea for a movie to do in Hong Kong (Chinese movie). So action! Action! Never wasting energy on worries and negative thoughts. I mean who has the most insecure job as I have? What do I live on? My faith in

You have a tendency to waste a lot of your energy in worry and anticipation. Remember... to enjoy your planning as well as your accomplishment, for life is too short for negative energy.

my ability that I'll make it. Sure my back screwed me up good for a year but with every adversity comes a blessing because a shock acts as a reminder to oneself that we must not get stale in routine.[6] Look at a rain storm; after its departure everything grows!

So remember that one who is possessed by worry not only lacks the poise to solve his own problems, but by his nervousness and irritability creates additional problems for those around him.

Well, what more can I say but damn that torpedo, full speed ahead!!

From a martial artist with a screwed up back but who has discovered a new powerful kick!

Bruce Lee

To Larry Hartsell[7]

June 6, 1971

Dear Larry,

How's your hip? I hope you're taking care of yourself.

I'll be doing a TV show [at] the end of this month. The show is called "Longstreet," a new TV series for this coming fall. The episode I'll be in is titled "The Way of the Intercepting Fist."

Nothing new developed with *Silent Flute*—it's a matter of

time. Am in the process of creating a new TV series based on martial art, hope it will turn out—will let you know.

I'll be on the cover of the next issue of *Black Belt*. Read it, you might find it interesting.

I've never met your family but do give them my best regards.
Take care my friend,
Bruce Lee

With this letter, Bruce enclosed one of his favorite poems, which praises the power of positive thinking in the face of adversity. It was sent as a motivational tool to strengthen his friend's will to recover:

If you think you are beaten, you are.
If you think you dare not, you don't.
If you like to win but think you can't
It is almost certain you won't.
If you think you will lose, you are lost.
For out of the world we find
Success BEGINS with a fellow's WILL.....
It's all in the state of mind.
If you think you're outclassed, you are.
You've got to think high to rise.
You've got to be sure of yourself before
You can ever win a prize.
Life's battles don't always go to
The stronger or faster man.
But sooner or later the man
Who wins is the man
WHO THINKS HE CAN!

To Leo Fong[8]

June 1971

Leo,
Just want to let you know I'll be very busy for the next four weeks, with rehearsing and shooting of the TV show "Longstreet." Immediately after that I'll be off to Hong Kong for four months where I'll be making two movies. Have to cancel Washington, DC trip.
Bruce

Bruce Lee works with James Franciscus on the set of the "Longstreet" TV series, ca. 1971.

To Leo Fong

July 10, 1971

Leo,
Finished shooting "Longstreet"—be sure to watch it in Sept. I did a good job on it.

In fact, Tom Tannenbaum, head of Paramount's TV department, has just contacted me for a development of a TV series for me. Also, he wants me to be a recurring character in Paramount's "Longstreet." This happens so fast I don't know what to think— must have done a good job!?

Am leaving for H.K. this Sunday morning to do two features—*The Big Boss*,[9] *King of Chinese Boxers* (can you believe this!!)—will be there for 4 months.

When I come back I'll be busy, with the possible shooting of *Silent Flute*, a movie (with Fred Weintraub) and the TV series we will be working with Paramount during my 4 months stay in Hong Kong—have to create a super martial art flick.

Have to prepare a lot of stuff—only two more days before I leave—well, what more can I say but that things are swinging my way.

B.

To Linda

Sent from the New Wanchai Hotel, Pakchong, Thailand, July 24, 1971, at 12:00 PM

Linda,

Bangkok was fine. However, Pakchong is something else. The mosquitoes are terrible and cockroaches are all over the place. Of course, the main reason for not having written is for lack of services, but also, I had a rather nasty accident—as I was washing a super thin glass, my grip broke the damn thing and cut my right hand rather deep—the worst cut I have, that requires ten stitches.

Don't worry though, I'm sure within two or three weeks I will be okayed, though it is inconvenient for me to write (or taking a bath or anything) for the past week.

I have yet [to] find out the confirmation of you people coming—though I am pretty damn sure. They want me to do a short film on JKD in exchange of your fare. I'm in no condition to do it but I'm sure they won't want to press matters because since my arrival, everyone, including the SHAW BRO. are calling and using all means to get me. One thing is for sure, I'm the super star in H.K. H.K. is having a typhoon sweeping over the city and I have [not] yet been able to confirm with Raymond Chow (the boss) on your matter of coming. To call U.S. is out of the question because [the phone] connection is terrible here.

I'm writing rather poorly due to my hand—it's much better

now—I'm taking my vitamin pills and though I'm down to 128 [pounds], I'm getting used to the condition here—the cockroaches are a constant threat, the lizards I can ignore—I just want you to know I miss all of you and am sending my love to you all. I'm looking forward to you coming. I don't think [they will] and I do hope they won't give me any problem.

Take care my love. I'll keep in touch and will tell you in more detail in my next letter.

Love and kisses,

Bruce

To Linda

Sent from the New Wanchai Hotel, Pakchong, Thailand

Linda,

By now you should have received my telegram or phone call (if the connection is clear and can be arranged). To begin with, Paramount wired for me to call Tom Tannenbaum—if I can get a good connection—anyway, another director (a fame lover) just arrived supposedly to take over the present director's job. It really doesn't matter, as long as he is capable as well as cooperative.

Well, what do you think of coming to Hong Kong to join me? As soon as I settle down, we will make the arrangement. In the meantime, find out all necessary information concerning the requirement of the trip.

The news in Hong Kong has been tremendous, though I have not yet been there. One thing that concerns me is the proper presentation with truth and sincerity, without leaning toward sensationalism.

The food in Bangkok is terrible, especially in Pakchong—this village has no beef and very little chicken and pork. Am I glad to [have] come with my vitamins.

I wish you were here because I miss you and the children a lot. This village is terrible, no place like home. I'm looking forward to meeting you in Hong Kong. By the way, have you received the check from Hong Kong? Do let me know and drop me a line at Pakchong.

My personal love to my wife, and Brandon & Shannon,

Bruce

P.S. Say hello to everybody.

To Linda

Sent from the New Wanchai Hotel, Pakchong, Thailand

Linda,

It's been 15 days since my arrival in Pakchong and it seems already like years! Due to lack of meat, I have to get canned meat for lunch. I'm glad I have brought along the vitamins.

I miss you a lot but Pakchong is no place for you and the children. It's an absolute under developed village with a big NOTHING.

The film I'm doing is quite amateur-like. A new director has replaced the uncertain old one; this new director is another so-so one with an almost unbearable air of superiority.

At any rate, I'm looking forward to leaving Pakchong to Bangkok, where it is at least half-way decent. Then I'll fly to Hong Kong and make the necessary arrangements for you people to come over—looking forward to seeing the three of you very much indeed.

My voice is gone (very hoarse!!) from yelling and talking under really terrible conditions—machine running, ice cutting, etc., etc. Anyway, all hell broke loose here. My back is getting along fair—need a lot of rest after a fight scene.

Have to go eat now—see if I can find any meat.

My love to you my dearest wife.

With kisses,

Bruce

To Linda

Sent from the New Wanchai Hotel, Pakchong, Thailand

Linda,

Though it was hard of hearing, it was nice talking to you on the phone. I [had] lost my voice and it was difficult for me to speak up. At any rate, it was very satisfying hearing your voice at this no man's land. Was it Brandon's voice that I heard?

Tried to call Tom Tannenbaum without any success. Will try again tonight.

I have a friend here. His name is Tavatachi Kosichroen. Could you get a brochure for him at the university regarding "Camera art?" Sort of an all-inclusive subjects on camera and movie making, etc. When you obtain the brochure, send it to:

Mr. Tavatchai Kosichroen
505 Friendship Village
Super Highway, Bangkok 10
Thailand

The shooting is picking up steam and is moving along much better than it was. The new director is no Roman Polanski but as a whole he is a better choice than our ex-director.

It looks like you will be coming to Hong Kong the beginning part of September—I'll be looking forward to seeing you at the airport.

At any rate, will be calling you when I arrive in Hong Kong.

According to everyone, I've lost a lot of weight, but I've been taking my vitamins and feel much better—more like an athlete!

Take care my wife.

Love to you and the children,

Bruce

To Linda

Sent from the New Wanchai Hotel, Pakchong, Thailand

My dearest wife,

Except for rotten hours—day and night shooting, Hong Kong film company is nice to work with.

Anyway, I feel that if we can, we should pay off the $3,000 on [the] house payment, preferably for, say, Dec. because (1) as of now, I feel I can earn some money from Paramount should I return to the States, say, in Sept. (2) H.K. film companies are hot after my work. I only hope we can get the extension. I should return with around $1500. Hold the 2 grand for Bob and Jim. *The Big Boss* is shaping up nicely as it moves along. This director is not bad after all, based on H.K. standard.

Bruce Lee with Lo Wei, director of The Big Boss, *during its filming in Pakchong, Thailand.*

Wouldn't it be bad IF Paramount's deal comes through, I would have to return straight from Bangkok and couldn't get any toys for my number one son Brandon?

I'm telling you, I'm the superstar in Hong Kong, with separate makeup, special chair, even separate Kleenex—yes. I feel strongly that I really can be the biggest ever in Hong Kong. It needs only careful planning in obtaining it.

When my pictures make a hit in Hong Kong, I'll start the minimum of (1) $10,000 a picture (2) ten percent interest (3) first-class round trip tickets and rooming for my full family.

Let's hope everything will move along nicely [from] Bangkok to U.S. and from U.S. our whole family goes to H.K. for 2 ½ months, Christmas and all.

Yes, it looks like this year is turning to some nice days ahead. My love to my distant wife,

Bruce

To Linda

Sent from the New Wanchai Hotel, Pakchong, Thailand

Linda,

I'm writing this letter to let you [know] that:

(A) "Longstreet" is such a success that reaction is instantaneous whenever my character comes up.

(B) So Paramount is asking me to reappear and stay as a re-occurrence character.

(C) So that means I MIGHT get a one month leave—after Sept. 5—and fly back to finish three more shows or whatever and then fly to Hong Kong with you and the kids to finish the second picture (*King of Chinese Boxers*).

(D) Of course, that means killing two birds with one stone and getting extra bread.

(E) I've already wired Tannenbaum for him to let me know of his "arrangement" for me.

In the meantime Tannenbaum is working on "Tiger Force."

Just a rush note to let you know what's happening. Looks like we might spend Christmas in H.K. together—unless something happens which I don't think [it will].

My love to you,

Bruce

(and to Brandon and Shannon)

To Linda

Sent from the New Wanchai Hotel, Pakchong, Thailand

By now you should have received my letter regarding (a) hoping to extend the loan or the second best way, whatever it might be (b) not to return Bob or James [their] loan as yet.

Received telegram from Paramount extracted as follows:

"Freelance offer for not less than three episodes at one thousand per episode. Each episode not to take more than three days from Sept. 5 to Sept. 30th... 1st Class round trip ticket... imperative we hear from you immediately to prepare script for the character you portray."

Well, here is my answer:

"My usual two thousand per episode plus quality technical advising. If acceptable can start work from Sept. 7 to Oct. 7. Notify immediately for schedule arrangement."

Really, if Paramount really likes me and if I really did such a good job, I feel I should advance to at least 2 grand per episode, disregard three days or anything.

Let's face it, my billing isn't exactly there. Who knows what the future holds? I feel rather definite about this, don't you? There comes a time when you have to advance or retreat—this time I can always retreat to my Hong Kong deal. At any rate, I have a feeling they would if I am valuable for "Longstreet."

Should be returning to Thai Hotel by the 17th or so of this month—will let you know, especially if Paramount replies, one way or the other.

Bruce

To Linda

Sent from the New Wanchai Hotel, Pakchong, Thailand

My dearest wife,
Today I've sent the telegram. However, it won't be till Monday [that] Tannenbaum will

Bruce Lee (center) *with members of the film crew for* The Big Boss.

receive it, unless there is extra service in the studio during the weekends.

Anyway, what it amounts to is a few more days of wondering how it will turn out. Disregard the consequences, I am firm on my ground of "it's about time to raise my worth." Well, it's a matter of whether I'm coming back to meet you and then [we] fly together to Hong Kong, or you and the kids flying over to meet me in Hong Kong. I have to say the first choice is more profitable and full of possibility. Time will tell.

Though I have to say the house-payment troubles me somewhat, I'm sure you will find the best possible way out. I hate to have an over all change of payment.

Anyway, my future in acting has now begun. I'm sure the one [the movie] I'm doing now will be a big success—again, time will tell.

Tomorrow begins the ending big fight. It will take over three days to shoot—that means we will leave Pakchong around the 17th—I will wire you when I return to [the] Thai hotel.

Though the place I'm in is utter hell, I'm in the profession where I belong and love to do.

Take care my love. It won't be long for us to get together.

Bruce

To Linda

Sent from the New Wanchai Hotel, Pakchong, Thailand

Linda,

Tomorrow and the following four days will be the big fight scene. After that, that is, after 15th of August, I'll be back to Thai Hotel. Otherwise, I'll notify you.

No news from Paramount. If I do not hear from them, I'll wire them before I leave Pakchong. Who knows what will happen? One thing is for certain, we will be traveling a lot in the Far East.

I'm looking forward to seeing you all very much—be it at the States or at Hong Kong airport. In the future, you can be sure you will be coming along. Tell Brandon when I go to Bangkok, I'll pick him up some toys and send them to him—unless the Paramount deal doesn't come through.

Have to rest early tonight—big fight scene coming up. Man, I'm tired from all the kicking and punching.

My love to my dearest,

Bruce.

To Linda

Sent from the New Wanchai Hotel, Pakchong, Thailand

Linda,

Have [a] free day tomorrow, which really is not saying too much. In a way, working occupies your mind in a place like Pakchong.

Haven't heard from Paramount—maybe Sept. is a little bit too late for returning for "Longstreet"—time will tell.

Can you send me some pictures of you and the children? The future looks extremely bright indeed, with lots of possibilities ahead—big possibilities. Like the song says "We've only just begun."

Today I've been to the set three times back and forth. If we're on schedule, we'll be moving to Bangkok to finish the picture.

Paramount hasn't contacted me so far. I have a feeling Stirling won't be able to finish the script for me to come back in Sept. At any rate, one way or other I really don't mind too much, the Lee family is enjoying some nice moment ahead.

My love to you my dearest.

My love to Brandon and little Shannie,

Bruce

To Linda

Sent from the New Wanchai Hotel, Pakchong, Thailand

My dearest wife,

Received your first letter and am happy to hear everything is fine. Yes, you and Brandon and Shannon are coming to Hong Kong. Just bring a few nice clothes for arrival and a few days out, for you will have a lot of new clothes made in Hong Kong.

Tom Tannenbaum wired for me to call him at his house over the weekend but I understand the connection is terrible here in Pakchong. So I wired him back to let him know and to have him call me instead. If you have not done so, give my Pakchong address to Stirling. Will be here for at least two more weeks before departure to Bangkok's Thai Hotel.

Golden Harvest is terribly shaken now for Shaw Brothers has been calling me and writing me for me to work with them instead. To keep in good term with me, that's why you are coming.

I'm anxious to hear what Tom Tannenbaum has to say—will

let you know or wire you if something GOOD does come about.

Amazing about Shannon's potty training—do give my love to Brandon and Shannon and tell them I'll see them at Hong Kong airport. Shape them up for I'm afraid there might be newspaper reporters at the airport.

I'm looking forward very much to seeing the three of you shortly—probably in Sept. or maybe August for I don't know what the crazy schedule is!? At any rate, I can tell you one thing—if done right, everything can be the best for us in Hong Kong.

In the mean time, may I say that the best still is having you, Brandon and Shannon.

My love to all of you,

Bruce

To Linda

Sent from the Thai Hotel, Bangkok, Thailand, on August 23, 1971, at 11:00 AM

August 22, 1971

Linda,

It's been raining a little bit here in Bangkok. I hope it won't hinder our shooting schedule. Two more weeks and I'll be home. In fact, I've made reservations for returning on the 6th of Sept. (Labor Day) Flight 846, arriving LA 10:45 in the morning. This will be the right flight unless I give you further notice of change.

Aside from all my physical problems, James Lee worries me somewhat. I hope he will snap out of it.

Have been shooting nights—from 6:30 to 4 AM. At least Bangkok has more facilities, but the mosquitoes are terrible!

Take care my dearest.

I love you. My love to the kids.

Bruce

To Linda

Sent from the Thai Hotel, Bangkok, Thailand, on August 23, 1971, at 11:00 AM

Bruce Lee devoted much thought to ways to raise the production standards of Hong Kong films.

Linda,

To make sure of [my] arriving [in] the States on time, I've gone through two days of hell. I sprained my ankle rather badly from a high jump on a slipped mattress—which required a drive of two hours to Bangkok to see a doctor—consequently I caught the flu (Bangkok is hot and stuffy and the traffic is a 24 hr. jam). Anyway, with fever, cold, aches and pain, we used close-up while I dragged my leg to finish the last fight.

I feel all right now, except for my ankle and am doing well in Bangkok. If the schedule is correct, we'll be returning to Hong Kong where I'll have one day of shooting and should be coming back on the 6th. I can tell you one thing, thing is happening too damn fast here.

Well, at least at Thai Hotel, I have breakfast in bed, nothing like Pakchong. By the way, I picked up a his and her "something" for both of us.[10] It's a surprise, for our anniversary. You will have to wait for me to bring them home to you.

Happy Anniversary! My sweet wife!

Love,

Bruce

Bruce enclosed a second letter, which was small and hand-printed, for Linda to give to Brandon:

Hello Brandon!

When I come back we will go to the toy shop.

Love you my son,

Dad

(P.S. Will you kiss Ma Ma and Shannon for me!?)

To Linda

Sent from the Thai Hotel, Bangkok, Thailand

Linda,

We were to shoot tonight, but the rain prevents us from doing so; therefore, it is rescheduled to shoot at 7 AM tomorrow morning.

By the way, I feel that with the Paramount deal, we should be able to make it comfortably to Hong Kong. Don't you think so? Of course, we have to worry about the tax.

In Hong Kong, Bruce and Linda celebrate Bruce's thirty-first birthday. The cake is decorated with an image of Bruce Lee from The Big Boss.

In fact, I'm going to ask for an advance from Tannenbaum on "Longstreet." Looks like we will be spending Christmas in Hong Kong.

If the schedule is on time, I'll be going to Hong Kong to do a reshooting of a certain scene, which will take around two days. Immediately [afterward] I'll be returning home.

Can't imagine that Shannon is making sentences already—she must be quite big by now. It seems ages since I left. At any rate, you will see my 7th anniversary gift—

a his and her present. Should have around one and a half grand when I return—I hope, anyway.

When everything works out I think you will enjoy this coming H.K. trip tremendously—I sure hope no mind-wrecking thing comes up.

Letters of the Dragon

I've written James Lee two letters; I hope he will write. He kind of worries me. Also, I think Bob might be able to join us on this trip.

Last but not least, I want you to know that the more places I go, the more people I meet, the more I come to appreciate you my dearest wife.

My love,

Bruce

To Ted Ashley, Warner Brothers Studios[11]

October 28th, 1971

Dear Ted,

I have talked to my lawyer Mr. Adrian Marshall about Warner's proposal. Since we are friends, I have chosen to write you directly.

In addition to our agreement we feel:

(a) that I should have a minimum of 4 months off a year to make features in Hong Kong.

(b) that I should have a participation in

(1) The TV series itself

(2) merchandising.

Shooting is running smoothly here and the last picture I made in Thailand has just been released and is on its way to break all records in Hong Kong—damn the torpedo, full speed ahead!

Take care and best regards to Linda.[12]

Peace,

Bruce

To Ted Ashley

Ted,
A personal short note to thank you and to tell you how much I appreciated your presence at the meeting.

Thank you, Ted.
Hello to Linda,
Bruce

To Ted Ashley

December 16th, 1971

Dear Ted,
I am sorry to hear about the outcome of "The Warrior." Well, you cannot win them all, but damn it, I am going to win one of these days.

Several things I [would] like to talk [about] with you:

(A) knowing my capability as an actor, plus the ever-increasing mentioning of martial art—which I always feel such "unique" and exciting action film has universal appeal—as well as the China situation, I feel Warner can definitely create a script, preferably for feature, tailored for me.

(B) I have started a film company (Concord) with a trusted friend of mine, and am looking forward very much to work with Warner on some future projects, or maybe Warner can help in releasing our future pictures in the States—like *A Fistful of Dollars* from Italy.

(C) In my commitment with Warner for "The Warrior" dating from Dec. 71 to Dec. 72, I think I have $25,000 coming to me. Warner can send it to my address [in] . . . Hong Kong.

Enclosed you will find some clippings which may or may not interest you, but more important still is the fact that I am daily improving in my acting and as a human being, and my dedication will definitely lead me to my goal. Any fair and rightful assistance from you will be deeply appreciated.

Again, thank you kindly for your kind participation on the initial stage of "The Warrior."

Take care my friend; my best regard to Linda, and may all be well.

Warmest regards,
Bruce

1972

To Siu Hon-san[13]

January 1972

Uncle Siu:

I have read your letter of 30 December. Thank you for your Golden Jubilee Memorial issue of Ching-wu school.

When I received your letter, the competition had ended. This is quite ironical. At this time I cannot go to Singapore because I have too much work to do. Personally, I certainly would have liked to have joined such a grand gathering. But now, everything is over.

This sounds a bit cold, but I have to emphasize once again that these words are from my heart. I hope that you can tell the Singapore National Pugilistic Federation that I am sorry.

Now I am preparing to shoot a new film, directed and acted by myself. Its aim is to promote the philosophy of martial arts. I hope that you elder masters can give me more advice and support!

In the end, if I have a chance, I will go to Singapore, to ask forgiveness from the elders!

With best wishes,

Bruce Lee

To Ted Ashley

March 22, 1972

Dear Ted,

Forgive me for not writing sooner as *Fist of Fury*, my second film, is being released presently, and is heading toward another all-time record . . . will confirm "when" the miracle happens.

Regarding our hope of a co-production with Warner, Mr. Raymond Chow and I are in the process of choosing carefully among projects that we have.

What more can I say but damn the torpedo, full speed ahead.

Warmest Regards,

Bruce Lee

To Ted Ashley

Dear Ted,

It was nice talking to you over the phone—sorry to hear about your car accident though! I hope you are in a state of better feeling, so here is what I have to say. I hope I will get a sincere and fair reply.

Presently, H.K. will be my base of operations as my films are enjoying "unbelievable" success, breaking all time records one after another.

Though one may say different locales have different tastes; however, "I'm positive" that something similar to what we have discussed prior to my going to H.K. will prove to be a success internationally. After all, action is action, and if Warner develops something specific for me, I'm sure my special brand of action will sock it to them. Of course, my experience in acting has grown considerably since "Longstreet" because I have gained from shouldering the responsibility of playing the leading role, plus directing my third film.

According to my partner, Raymond Chow, Aubrey and Netting are coming to H.K. in August to discuss about co-productions—film ventures starring me. Also, an independent, American producer here is in the process of negotiating with me to produce films in English for international release.

Financially, I am secure; unheard of offers have been made to me. Ted, I have gone through the interesting experience of being Number One in Mandarin films. Fame and fortune, and I mean by any standards, are mine. I would like to feel you would not interpret this as an ego trip, for after this swift and unexpected adjustment, I have found, after much soul searching, that deep down what I honestly value more than anything else is quality: doing one's best in the manner of the responsibility and craftsmanship of a Number One.

So Ted, from one human being to another, and I am saying it simply and directly, "I honestly feel that this diligently trained body plus a time tried realistic faith in knowing that I CAN. . ." will undoubtedly make it and make it in a really big way should this Chinaman get a fair seeing and fair support from someone.

Despite all the privileges, there is one unavoidable frustration: Hong Kong film industry is definitely behind in quality as compared to other leading countries. The way I look at it, and honestly feel it, is that this Chinaman will definitely invade the States in a big way, one way or another. I am sure, if you give this matter a fair and serious thought, something will be worked out to our mutual benefit. Should this project come through, we, as good friends, will enjoy it that much more.

I don't think I'll be moving for a couple of weeks yet; at any rate, I'll notify your local manager Robert Chan regarding my whereabouts. By the way, [as for] any information regarding this possible project, Robert Chan can definitely keep you up to date.

Looking forward very much to hearing from you next week on your honest and fair decision one way or the other. My current phone number is K856576 and I have left word to page me at the studio (K250136).

Take good care of yourself.

Your friend,

Bruce

To "John"[14]

Dear John,

You hit the nail right on the head. I've just been back from a dubbing session—busy is the word!!

Sincerity seems to be part of your make-up and though we've not been together for too long, my immediate reply to you is as follows: (a) time wise I wouldn't have time to teach, but I'm willing—when time permits—to honestly express or "to open myself" to you, to act as sort of a sign pole for a traveler.

Bruce Lee and his boyhood friend Siu Kee Lun ("Little Unicorn," right) discuss a point of filmmaking. Hong Kong, 1972

My experience will help, but I insist and maintain that art—true art that is—cannot be handed out. Furthermore, art is never decoration or embellishment. Instead it is a constant process of maturING (in the sense of NOT [having] arrived!).

You see, John, when we have the opportunity of working out, you'll see that your way of thinking is definitely not the same as mine. Art, after all, is a means of acquiring "personal" liberty. Your way is not my way nor mine yours.

So whether or not we can get together, remember well that art "LIVES" where absolute freedom is. With all the training thrown to nowhere, with a mind (if there is such a verbal substance) perfectly unaware of its own working, with the "self" vanishing [into] nowhere the art of JKD attains its perfection.

I have to hit the sack now 'cause I have to work early tomorrow plus training afterwards. This is just a short note to a fellow martial artist.

"The process of becoming,"

Bruce

To Mito Uyehara

August 12, 1972

Mito,

You son of a gun! Sending that plaque of "Hall of Fame" was indeed a great surprise and I really am not knowing what my honest reaction toward such title is. In fact I once remembered asking you not to put me on the list should such voting be in.

Frankly, such plaque is to me like nothing; however, as a human being and particularly as a friend, I thank you and appreciate your offering. I would like to think this plaque is some sort of "honest" universal appraisal toward a "doer." If my attitude seems less enthusiastic toward receiving the plaque than others, do pardon my stubbornness. You should know me by now.

After reading your article on me, I have mixed feelings. To many, the word "success" seems to be a paradise, but now that I'm in the midst of it, it is nothing but circumstances that seem to complicate my innate feeling toward simplicity and privacy. I am saying this because, Mito, you are my friend, so I feel like "letting it out."

Yet, whether I like it or not, circumstances are thrust upon me and being a fighter at heart I sort of fight it in the beginning but soon realize what I need is not inner resistance and needless conflict (in the form of dissipation); rather, by joining forces to readjust and make the best of it.

I couldn't go wrong because what I always like about myself is this stickability toward quality and the sincere desire to do it right. In a way, I am glad that this prosperous happening is occurring to me when I am maturing to a state of readiness and definitely will not blow it because of "self-glorification" or [being] "blinded by illusions." I am prepared.

Believe me, this man here is confronting some "real" pressure and needless to say it is easier said than done. After all, fame and fortune are illusive creations and impostors. So hell with it and steering my direction and unperturbedly I try to march on.

Well, my dear friend—lately "friend" has come to be a scarce word, a sickening game of watchfulness toward offered friendships—I miss you and our once simple lunches together and our many joyful communications.

Take care and have fun—hope you are still jogging, which is the only form of relaxation to me nowadays.

Bruce

To Linda

Linda,

Am going to see a movie technically advised by Unicorn—probably another "moon cake" (sound in Chinese, means "most boring").[15] At any rate, will meet with Unicorn's director afterwards to make sure he doesn't get screwed by [offering] more of my advice and ideas on the script—probably ending up with me showing how to do it.

Have been working on ["southern fist/northern leg"] script and am definitely somewhere in ninth heaven.

Will call should the talk go to dinner stage—running is in my plan today, though I'm sore.

Love to you,

Bruce

P.S. Better stand by for Shui King.

To Jhoon Goo Rhee

Dear Jhoon,

The premier of my new film in Hong Kong has been rescheduled for December 23.[16] Also, I have talked to Mr. Raymond Chow and although a definite idea has not been formed, I think there is this possibility of making a film entitled *Tae Kwon Do*.

And I think, personally, it will do you a world of good to be the first one to do it and also for public recognition.

I will write again as more developments come about, but do notice that the premier night of the film has been rescheduled.

Take care,
Bruce

To "Unicorn"

November 1972

Unicorn my friend,

Sometimes when you are all alone by yourself sitting down and listening to music, without realizing it you begin to imagine, and you begin to form in your heart [a clear vision] about the fundamental source of martial art, the fundamental source of life, and the fundamental source of martial art films. The three elements together become one and they each inspire the other to enable you to understand any one aspect's true fundamentality and source.

When you're faced with looking at your own life with awakened eyes, you will have increased a bit in the knowledge of yourself (in other words, your mental and physical abilities will become clear to you) and knowledge of anything outside of yourself is only superficial and very shallow. To put it another way, self knowledge has a liberating quality.

Bruce Lee on the set of The Unicorn Fist *in 1972. Lee choreographed the action for his friend "Little Unicorn" (left).*

One additional comment: The energy from within and the physical strength from your body can guide you toward accomplishing your purpose in life—and to actually act on actualizing your duty to yourself.

Notes

1. On January 29, 1971, Bruce Lee left Los Angeles for India to scout locations for *The Silent Flute*, a film he intended to make. Accompanying him were Hollywood superstar James Coburn and Academy Award–winning screenwriter Stirling Silliphant, both students of his. They arrived in New Delhi, India, on Monday, February 1, 1971, and scouted locations until Thursday, February 11, 1971. During this ten-day period, while driving across the Indian desert, Bruce found time to write the following letter.

2. There is no date on this letter, but in all probability it was written in March or April 1971. (*Black Belt* magazine published the article mentioned in their September 1971 edition.)

3. A book by Frederick Perls, the Gestalt-therapy pioneer, several of whose books Bruce Lee had in his library.

4. Leo Fong sent a five-volume course-on-drawing book to Bruce.

5. Bruce Lee's idea, which he entitled "The Warrior," eventually became the "Kung Fu" television series. The executives at Warner Brothers, however, felt that he was "too Asian" to carry the lead on an "American" (Lee was an American) TV series and so gave the lead role to Caucasian actor David Carradine.

6. Between 1964 and 1970, Bruce Lee hurt his back several times. The severest of these injuries (or, perhaps, reinjuries) came as a result of a weight-training accident in which he neglected to warm up sufficiently before performing a very strenuous lower back exercise. As a result, he damaged the fourth sacral nerve in his lower back. His doctors told him that he would never be able to perform martial art again, but he persevered, and eventually not only recovered his previous level of skill and conditioning, but actually surpassed it! Nevertheless, he was plagued by back pain for the remainder of his life.

7. Larry Hartsell was one of Bruce Lee's students at his Los Angeles Chinatown school. Hartsell had suffered a severe hip injury during an automobile accident in October 1970. Bruce Lee visited him in the hospital on five separate occasions and then wrote him this follow-up letter of support. The poem attached meant a great deal to Bruce during his own period of rehabilitation, after a severe back injury almost ended his martial art career. He had a typed copy of it permaplaqued and hung on the wall of his office, and he would refer to it whenever he faced great physical, economic, or career hardships.

8. After many months of severe financial adversity, Bruce Lee received a long-distance phone call from Hong Kong film producer Raymond Chow. Chow said that he was starting a new film production company called Golden Harvest Films, and that he wanted to sign Bruce Lee to a two-picture deal. Realizing that if he were given a vehicle to express himself cinematically, he would be well on his way to establishing himself as a major theatrical talent and a bankable actor, Bruce Lee accepted what, in retrospect, was Chow's minuscule offer of $15,000 for two films.

9. The first of Bruce Lee's two films for Golden Harvest Films was called *The Big Boss*.

10. The "his and her something" that Bruce picked up was a pair of rings.

11. Ted Ashley was the chairman of Warner Brothers Films, and occasional student of Bruce Lee's.

12. Ted Ashley's wife, Linda Ashley.

13. This is Bruce Lee's reply to Siu Hon-san's letter requesting his presence at a gathering of martial artists in Singapore. Unfortunately, Bruce Lee received the invitation too late to attend.

14. The identity of the addressee is unknown. There is no date on the letter, but its reference to a dubbing session probably refers to *The Way of the Dragon*. Lee was very active in overseeing all aspects of its production, including the dubbing, which was done during the summer of 1972.

15. One of Bruce Lee's oldest and closest friends in Hong Kong was the Chinese actor Siu Kee Lun—"Unicorn" to his friends. Like Bruce Lee's father, Unicorn's father was an actor in the Cantonese opera. Unicorn later appeared in two of Bruce Lee's feature films, *Fist of Fury* and *The Way of the Dragon*.

16. There is no date on this letter, but it was probably written between September and November 1972, as *The Way of the Dragon* premiered December 23, 1972.

July 20, 1973.

Adrian Marshall
Suite 920, Century City
10100 Santa Monica Blvd.
Los Angeles, Calif. 90067
U.S.A.

Dear Adrian,

Will be arriving Los Angeles on Aug. 3rd, would like to sit down and hope you can leave open the weekend of Aug. 4th to 5th to discuss the followings:

1/ the deal with Hana Barbera

2/ Warner's proposition

3/ Titanas from Italy

4/ Andy's proposition from H.K. which I will explain to you when I see you in person

All in all, it will be a hectic schedule with television shows, United Press interview etc., spending one week in L.S. and leaving on Aug. 18th to New York for another week of publicity, maybe Johnny Carson Show and so forth etc. And then, my publicity tour will officially end on Aug. 24th and on Aug. 25th I will meet Linda at L.A., ready to come back to H.K. hopefully in one piece.

In the meantime, if there is any preliminary discussions that you can start without my presence, go right ahead. However, I would prefer you and I sit down first and discuss the whole plan of the income tax situation before we proceed on. Also, I would like to meet with you first before meeting with Raymond Chow and then both of us will hear him out. By the way, there are also other propositions of books, clothings, endorsements etc. At any rate, I will talk to you personally when I see you.

Take care my friend,

Very truly yours,

Bruce

PS: Looking forward to a sincere opened and honest relationship between you and I to really do something fair and square. By the way, SY Weintraub had just called and will be flying here to H.K., supposedly to have devised a super plan for me. At any rate, I won't sign anything until I and then maybe Raymond and/or SY sit down and we all talked. So get prepared !! See you soon.

Part 5

THE
FINAL
YEAR

(1973)

To Jon Y. Lee[1*]

Posted from Kowloon, Hong Kong, on January 9, 1973, at 10:00 AM

January 9, 1973

Dear Jon,

How ironical it is to write you [that] I received a letter from James, that "lovable bastard," on the day of Greg's call.

He sent me a birthday card saying "Friends like you, comes once in a blue moon." Well, what more can I say but I have lost one [dear friend]—who knows you . . . understands you.

James was my student, yet he was more a friend. I am glad in one thing though, and this I know, since our friendship we both have benefited from our ups and downs. He was a man and I love him. You understand Jon, I have lost a brother. I, too, respect him with all his faults and good merits.

Let me know if I can be of any help. I can't write further.

Bruce

P.S. He was a fighter. Consider the odds!! He kept blasting!

To Jon Y. Lee

Jon,

Thank you for your kind letter, Jon. James might be stubborn, but he was a good man in my book. He might not have been too neat or too orderly, but he never consciously meant harm. He had a temper but he knew what was right.

I, Bruce Lee, have another loss, and that loss is one I can never replace.

Bruce

---

*Notes for Part 5 are on page 184.

To Jhoon Goo Rhee

February 9, 1973

Dear Jhoon,
I am at Mr. Chow's office at the moment, and both Mr. Chow and I are waiting for the picture of your student that you have promised to send previously.

Mr. Chow has already told his associate to work on the script while I am very busy working in the Warner Brothers picture.

So would you please then rush me those photos so that I can present them to Mr. Chow along with whatever suggestions you would like to make on this possible project together.

Bruce Lee talks with his production partner Raymond Chow (right) during a break in filiming The Game of Death, *ca. 1972.*

I am doing fine—no! I should say "excellent." You know how it is. It's so damned good that I cannot bear it. Lots of luck and take care of your knee. A Korean without a good knee is a dead Korean.

Warmest personal regards,
Sincerely yours,
Bruce Lee

To Ted Ashley

April 22, 1973

Ted,

Nowadays, my offers for doing a film have reached to the point which I guarantee you will both surprise as well as shock you.

Viewing from the angle of efficient practical business sense, I hope we will be fair and square and have mutual trust and confidence—I have had a bad experience doing a picture with some person or organization in Hong Kong. In other words, I was burned once, and didn't like it.

Without Bruce Lee, I am sure that Warner Bros. will definitely and factually suffer no loss, and vice versa; therefore, and I sincerely mean it, that is from one human being to another, practical business or whatever it is, I sincerely hope that during this meeting, I will find a genuine and truthful friend, Ted Ashley.

As a friend, I am sure you agree with me that, after all, quality, extremely hard work, and professionalism is what cinema is all about. My twenty years of experience, both in martial arts and acting, has apparently led to the successful harmony of appropriateness of showmanship and genuine, efficient, artful expression. In short, this is it and ain't nobody knows it like I know it. Pardon my bluntness, but that is me!

Under such circumstances, I sincerely hope that you will open up the genuineness within you and be absolutely fair and square in our transactions. Because of our friendship, I am holding up my money-making time—like ten offers from hungry producers—to look forward to this meeting. You see, Ted, my obsession is to make, pardon the expression, the fuckingest action motion picture that has ever been made.

In closing, I will give you my heart, but please do not give me your head only; in return, I, Bruce Lee, will always feel the deepest appreciation for the intensity of your involvement.

Bruce Lee

To Ted Ashley

Ted,
Thank [the] Lord that I talked to Dick Ma. A few current up to date thoughts and emotions:

(1) I'm ready for action—preparing several [projects] in the meantime, ready to go anytime, anywhere.

Bruce Lee giving directions to cast and crew on the set of Enter the Dragon, ca. 1973.

(2) I'm sending *The Way of the Dragon* for your advice whether or not or how it should be released.

All in all, I'm having a burden of nothing to do—raring to go. Whatever. . . .

Talk to you later, but do think of the possibilities—they will be great!!

Bruce

To Taky Kimura[2]

May 1973

Taky,
In life there are the pluses and the minuses, and it is time for you to concentrate on the pluses. It might be difficult but fortunately for us human beings, we have self-will. Well, it is time to employ it.

Life is an ever-flowing process and somewhere on the path some unpleasant things will pop up—it might leave a scar, but then life is flowing on and like running water, when it stops, it grows stale. Go bravely on, my friend, because each experience teaches us a lesson, and remember, if there is anything at all I can help with, let me know.

Keep blasting because James Lee did, and life is such that sometimes it is nice and sometimes it is not.

Take care,

Bruce

Bruce Lee had planned to portray certain significant historical Chinese heroes in future films. He went so far as to be fitted for period costumes, such as the one shown here, ca. 1973.

To James Coburn[3]

June 13, 1973

Jim,

Missed you when I was in Los Angeles, but had left that super duper outfit at your house. Hope you like it. Everything is cool here. Spoke to Stirling and I told him that between you and him I'll thrust our silent flute in your hands.

Might be coming back for the opening. We have that artist who did *Dirty Harry* and "Mission Impossible," to score the music for the Warner Brothers picture.[4] Also another added [piece of] good news is that we'll have a summer release at the Chinese Grauman Theater.

All my best and keep cool

Bruce

P.S. Say hello to Beverly.

To Ted Ashley

Posted from the Hyatt Regency, Kowloon, Hong Kong

June 1973

Dear Ted,

Just a note to let you know that this "18 year old" has arrived safely.[5]

Do consider carefully in regard to the title of *Enter the Dragon*.

1. This "unique" dragon (the Chinese, the spiritual, etc.) is not one of those Won Ton Kung Fu flicks from H.K.
2. With the rightful publicity we can tell on the screen as well as outside that this dragon has broken the all-time record consecutively—like you said, "it comes across."

I really think this is a good title and like I said, do think it over carefully because "Enter the Dragon" suggests the emergence (the entrance) of someone (a personality) that is of quality.

Time is pressing, Ted.

Do please send me the two scripts so I can work it over.

Warmest personal regards,

Bruce Lee

(The Dragon in Chinese, by the way)

To Run Run Shaw[6]

Dear Run Run,

As of now, consider September, Oct. & November, a period of three months, reserved for Shaw.

    Specific terms [we] will discuss upon my arrival.

    Bruce Lee

To Adrian Marshall—Bruce Lee's last letter

Despite his hard-won success, Lee's primary concern was always a full commitment to quality, which explains why his films have withstood the test of time and have become classics of the genre.

Bruce Lee's last letter was written to his attorney, Adrian Marshall. Bruce wrote it on the last day of his life and posted it several hours before his death. Due to the distance between Hong Kong and Los Angeles, the letter arrived on Marshall's desk a week later. "It was an eerie feeling to receive Bruce's letter seven days after he passed away," Marshall says. "However, I thought readers might be interested in learning what promise the future had for Bruce at this particular period in his life." In the missive, Bruce outlines his various business offers and plans for the future. To my (and Marshall's) knowledge, this is the last letter Bruce Lee ever wrote.

July 20, 1973

Dear Adrian,

Will be arriving Los Angeles on Aug. 3rd, would like to sit down and hope you can leave open the weekend of Aug. 4th to 5th to discuss the following:

1/ the deal with Hanna Barbera
2/ Warner's proposition
3/ Titanas from Italy
4/ Andy's proposition from H.K. which I will explain to you when I see you in person.

All in all, it will be a hectic schedule with television shows, United Press interview, etc., spending one week in LA and leaving on Aug. 18th to New York for another week of publicity, maybe[the] "Johnny Carson Show" and so forth, etc. And then, my publicity tour will officially end on Aug. 24th and on Aug. 25th I will meet Linda at LA, ready to come back to H.K. hopefully in one piece.

In the meantime, if there is any preliminary discussions that you can start without my presence, go right ahead. However, I would prefer you and I sit down first and discuss the whole plan of the income tax situation before we proceed on. Also, I would like to meet with you first before meeting with Raymond Chow and then both of us will hear him out. By the way, there are also other propositions of books, clothing, endorsements, etc. At any rate, I will talk to you personally when I see you.

Take care my friend.

Very truly yours,

Bruce

P.S. Looking forward to a sincere open and honest relationship between you and I to really do something fair and square. By the way, Sy Weintraub had just called and will be flying here to H.K., supposedly to have devised a super plan for me. At any rate, I won't sign anything until I and then maybe Raymond and/or Sy sit down and we all [have] talked. So get prepared!! See you soon.

Notes

1. Jon Yimm Lee was the brother of James Yimm Lee. This letter was written when Bruce Lee received news of James's death from his son, Greg. As far back 1971, Bruce was growing increasingly concerned about James's deteriorating health, and, indeed, deeply felt the loss of his friend and JKD comrade.

2. Bruce Lee wrote this letter when he heard that Kimura had recently split up with his wife. The original letter has been lost, but the passage reprinted here has been preserved by inclusion in several books published in the mid-1970s.

3. American actor James Coburn was one of Bruce Lee's private students and had collaborated with him and Stirling Silliphant on the *Silent Flute* screenplay about the higher principles of martial art. Bruce Lee wrote this letter upon his return to Hong Kong from Los Angeles, where he had attended a rough screening of his final film, *Enter the Dragon,* at the Warner Brothers studios.

4. The artist is composer Lalo Schifrin.

5. Bruce Lee wrote this letter shortly after returning to Hong Kong from America, where he had undergone a battery of physical tests, was given a "clean bill of health," and told he "had the body of an 18-year old." Sadly, he passed away thirty days later from a cerebral edema.

6. Sir Run Run Shaw is the driving force behind Shaw Brothers Films in Hong Kong, which, until Bruce Lee put Golden Harvest Films on the map, was the undisputed leader of Southeast Asian filmmakers. Shaw had been courting Bruce Lee since 1971, but Bruce and Raymond Chow formed a successful partnership in 1972. Always interested in broadening his experience, Bruce contemplated making a variety of films with other producers. This letter indicates that he was intending to make at least one movie with Shaw Brothers in the fall of 1973.

INDEX

Numbers in *italics* indicate pages on which pictures are found.

A lowercase *n* indicates that the reference is found in the Notes under the number that follows the *n*.

TO THE READER

A portion of the proceeds derived from the sale of this book will go to benefit both the Bruce Lee & Brandon Lee Medical Scholarship Endowment at the University of Arkansas and the Brandon Bruce Lee Drama Scholarship at Whitman College in Walla Walla, Washington. If you would like to make your own contribution to these two very worthy causes, we encourage you to write or call:

University of Arkansas

4301 West Markham #716
Little Rock, AK 72205–7199
(501) 686–7950

Whitman College

Development Office
Walla Walla, WA 99362
(509) 527–5165

For further authentic information on Bruce Lee or the art and philosophy of Jun Fan jeet kune do, please write to:

The Jun Fan Jeet Kune Do Nucleus

967 E. Parkcenter Boulevard
Box 177
Boise, Idaho 83706